IN PERFORMANCE

Contemporary Monologues
for Men and Women
Late Twenties to Thirties

JV Mercanti

Applause Theatre & Cinema Books
An Imprint of Hal Leonard Corporation

Published in 2014 by Applause Theatre & Cinema Books
An Imprint of Hal Leonard Corporation
7777 West Bluemound Road
Milwaukee, WI 53213

Trade Book Division Editorial Offices
33 Plymouth St., Montclair, NJ 07042

Permissions can be found on page 235, which constitutes an extension of this copyright page.

Printed in the United States of America

Book design by Mark Lerner

Library of Congress Cataloging-in-Publication Data

In performance : contemporary monologues for men and women late twenties to thirties / [edited by] J V Mercanti.
    pages cm
  ISBN 978-1-4803-6747-0
1. Monologues. 2. Acting–Auditions. I. Mercanti, J. V., editor of compilation.
  PN2080.I5225 2014
  808.82'45–dc23
                          2014025806

www.applausebooks.com

CONTENTS

MEN'S MONOLOGUES

WOMEN'S MONOLOGUES

PREFACE

One of the best auditions I've ever seen was for Roundabout Theatre Company's 2001 revival of Stephen Sondheim and James Goldman's musical *Follies*. Jim Carnahan, the casting director, and I had called in Judith Ivey for the role of Sally Durant Plummer. If you don't know who Judith Ivey is, please Google her immediately. You have most likely seen her in something on stage, in film, or on television. You might also have seen a production that she's directed. She is a prolific artist.

The role of Sally Durant Plummer is fragile and complex. Sally has been married to Buddy for years, but all that time she has been pining for the love of Ben Stone, who is (unhappily) married to Sally's former best friend, Phyllis. Sally is going crazy with love and desire that has been burning for over twenty years.

Ms. Ivey was asked to prepare a cut from Sally's famous first-act song "In Buddy's Eyes," an aria through which she tries to convince Ben, in order to make him jealous, that she's deliriously happy in her life with Buddy. She was also asked to prepare a short scene from the show. Present in the room for the audition were Stephen Sondheim, the composer and lyricist; Matthew Warchus, the director; Todd Haimes, artistic director; Jim Carnahan, casting director; Paul Ford, the accompanist; a reader; and myself.

Walking into the room as herself, Ms. Ivey conversed with Mr. Warchus and Mr. Sondheim about her career and, very briefly, about the character. She then took a moment with Paul Ford to discuss the music. Following that, she came to the center of the playing space, closed her eyes, took a deep breath, and prepared herself to begin acting. In that moment of preparation, which truly lasted no longer than a breath, her body changed, her physicality changed, the very air around her seemed to change. She took the character into her body. Ms. Ivey then opened her eyes, nodded at Mr. Ford, and began to sing.

Ms. Ivey executed the song with specificity, a rich but contained emotional connection to the material, a strong objective, carefully thought-out actions, and a deep understanding of this woman and her desire. She went directly from the song to the scene, completely off-book (lines memorized), and when she finished — the room was silent. Mr. Sondheim had tears in his eyes. Mr. Warchus didn't have a word of direction to give her. It was not that Ms. Ivey had provided us with a complete performance. No, not at all. She had shown us the possibility of what she could create. She had shown us the potential of her Sally Durant Plummer. Her point of view was clear, consistent, and deeply, deeply affecting.

"Thank you, Judith. That was wonderful," Matthew Warchus finally said.

"I really love Sally," she responded, "But I was wondering if you might also consider me for the role of Phyllis. I've prepared that material as well."

"Of course I would. Would you like a few minutes to go outside and prepare?" he asked.

"No. No, that's all right. I can do it right now," she responded.

And after saying this, Ms. Ivey closed her eyes. She very slowly turned away from us, put her hair up in a tight bun, and turned around to face the room. It took no longer than thirty seconds, but once again her body, her posture, the way she related to the air around her, had changed. The atmosphere of the room shifted with her. Once again, she nodded to Paul Ford at the piano, and she fearlessly launched into the Phyllis Stone material.

It was astonishing. Not a false note was sung or uttered. Ivey had such a deep understanding of the cold facade Phyllis wears in order to cover up her broken heart and broken dreams. Phyllis is the polar opposite of Sally: cool, controlled, calculating, and hard.

Ms. Ivey thanked us for the opportunity. We thanked her for her work. The room remained still and silent for a while after she left.

Without a doubt, Mr. Warchus knew he must cast her in the show. She landed the role of Sally Durant Plummer.

It was clear that Ms. Ivey did a very thorough study of the text in preparation for this audition. She understood who these characters were at their very core; how they thought; why they spoke the way they did, using language in their own individual and specific way. She understood how they moved, where they held their weight, how they related to the space around them. Most importantly, she understood the characters' objectives (what they wanted) and how to use the other person in the scene to get what she wanted. Finally, Ivey was excited to show us how she could portray these women. She wasn't concerned about getting it "right." She managed to accomplish this while bringing herself to the character instead of the other way around.

More recently, I was casting the Broadway revival of *Romeo and Juliet* starring Orlando Bloom and Condola Rashād. The process of making this production happen is a book in and of itself. It was in development for over three years.

I flew to Los Angeles to work with Mr. Bloom in June 2012. We spent a week going through the text, talking about objectives, tactics, and actions. We defined Romeo's main objective, simply, as "to fly towards the sun." Then we discussed his relationship with the other characters in the play and how they connected to this objective.

Wait. Why isn't his objective about Juliet, you ask? His super-objective cannot be about Juliet, because, upon Romeo's first entrance in the play, he hasn't even *seen* her yet. He can't come on stage playing to win someone he doesn't even know. But if you perform a careful analysis of the text, you will find a plethora of both sun and flying imagery. Once he finds Juliet, she becomes his sun. This is why it's helpful as an actor to jot down the recurring themes or images you come across when reading a play you're working on, even if you're only focusing on a monologue from a larger text. This is also why it's important to pay attention to the *words* the playwright uses.

Bloom is a physical actor, and we spent a lot of time playing on our feet, finding the scenes through physical action as well as language. Getting Romeo into his body helped get Bloom out of his head. Also, the very simple and stimulating objective—to fly toward the sun—gave him a place to start from that sparked his imagination, was very actable, and influenced his physical life. His heart was always open and reaching up.

I worked with Bloom again in NYC for a few days, and then he flew to London to audition for David Leveaux, our director. He landed the role. That was in July 2012. Now we had to cast the rest of the play.

We did an initial round of casting in July and August of that year, seeing actors for a variety of the supporting roles. As we were securing official dates (as well as a Juliet!), we could only audition actors and tell them we were interested in them. We couldn't make offers. We couldn't tell them actual production dates. We couldn't tell them anything for certain, not even who our Romeo was. Many of these actors were not officially called back until January 2013, which is when Ms. Rashād (whose first audition was in August) landed the Juliet role after four auditions in New York and one in Los Angeles with Bloom.

Some actors were cast on the merit of their first audition six months before, no callback necessary. I was in constant contact with agents and managers from July 2012 to May 2013, letting them know we were still interested in their clients; that there might or might not be another round of callbacks; that they should let me know immediately if their client had another job offer, et cetera. At the same time, I was auditioning new people for parts we hadn't seen earlier. The show required a cast of twenty-three on-stage actors and one off-stage standby for Bloom.

Putting the Capulet and Montague families together was like a puzzle: headshots spread out on a long folding table as we weighed the pros of each actor, their look, and their qualities. All of these factors influence the production as a whole. Official offers were not made until May 2013.

I tell you this to illustrate how you, the actor, never know what goes on behind the scenes. Ultimately, you have no power over it. The only power you have is how you present yourself to the room as a person and a performer.

With rehearsal quickly approaching in July 2013, we had one role left to cast: Sampson, a servant of the House of Capulet. The actor playing this part would also understudy Justin Guarini, who played Paris. By the time we were in final callbacks for this small role, I had prescreened (an audition with just the actor and casting director, preceding a director's callback) or checked the availability of some four hundred actors for the part. Four hundred actors for a role that had approximately three lines of dialogue.

David Leveaux is attracted to actors who have strong, specific personalities and who bring that into the room. The male casting for this production depended on virile, strong, playful men who also happened to be skilled in speaking verse, as David puts it, "on the line." That means speaking the lines as written and not adding unnecessary pauses or breaks in between every thought or word, allowing the action of the line to take you to the poetry instead of vice versa.

Our Sampson, a young man by the name of Donte Bonner, was all of these things and more. He walked into the room calm, collected, and in control. He enjoyed the process of auditioning. Bonner was excited to show us what he could do with the role, not preoccupied with hoping we liked him. This attitude is immediately attractive in an actor. On top of this, Bonner brought his own, unique point of view to the character he was reading for. He was simple, specific and alive. He was also skilled at taking direction. Although he had a very strong idea of his own, he was able to adjust when David asked for something completely different.

You can achieve the same level of performance as Ms. Ivey or Mr. Bonner if you put the requisite amount of work into your monologue, ask yourself the right questions (and the questions I ask you to examine following each of the pieces in this book), and activate your imagination.

Introduction
Approaching the Monologue

Actors are interpretive storytellers. We often forget that.

You take the words the writer has given you and process them through your own unique instrument (your mind, your body, your imagination, and, hopefully, your heart and your soul), and you turn those words into action—into doing. I'm sure you've been taught by this point in your career that acting is doing. As a teacher, acting coach, and director, I am constantly asking the questions "What are you doing?" and "Why are you doing that?" This doesn't mean a *physical* action. It means how are you *actively pursuing* your objective?

I'm also always asking the question "What does that mean?"

Most beginning actors think that memorizing the lines is enough. Or that emoting is enough. As I tell my undergraduate students, acting is hard work, and it's more than just memorizing lines and saying them out loud. It takes emotional connection, analytical skill, and an understanding of human behavior and relationships—as well as a relationship with language—to turn the written word into honest, believable action. Remember, any playwright worth his/her salt takes great care in choosing the language a character uses. In a well-written play, each character speaks differently. It is your job to find the key to unlocking the meaning of that language while giving it your own personal spin.

Rehearsing a monologue is tricky business, because you don't physically have a partner in front of you to work off of, react to, and actually affect. Oftentimes you'll find yourself staring at an empty chair, saying the lines out loud over and over. Hopefully, what follows will help you deepen your rehearsal process and activate your imagination. Imagination is one of the strongest tools an actor can possess. If you can enter a room and create a specific, believable world in two minutes, we will trust that you can sustain that world for two-plus hours on a stage or in front of a camera.

You're reading this book because you're looking for an audition piece. It might be for a nonequity or community-theater production, an undergraduate or graduate program, or a professional meeting with an agent or casting director. It may even be for an EPA.[1] Whatever the case, you're looking for a piece that—I hope—you feel you connect with on some level; that expresses a particular essence of you; that shows off your sense of humor or sense of self; and that, above all, tells a story you want to tell.

Your monologue choice tells the person (or sometimes the numerous people) behind the table something about you. Certainly it lets us know that you can stand in front of an audience, comfortable in your own body, and perform. It tells us you can open your mouth and speak someone else's words with meaning,

---

1   EPA stands for Equity Principal Auditions. All productions that produce on a contract with Actors Equity Association are required to have these calls. The casting department for these EPAs can provide scenes from the play they are casting or request monologues.

confidence, and a sense of ease. It lets us know whether or not you have the ability to project or modify your voice depending on the requirements of the space.

More than that, your monologue choice tells us something about who you are as a person. Your monologue can tell us the type of things you respond to emotionally, intellectually, and humorously. After all, we're going under the assumption that you put a lot of time and care into finding a piece that you wanted to perform. You took the time to commit that piece to memory and to heart. You've imbued it with your sense of humor, understanding, compassion, pain, and so on. More than just telling us whether or not you can act—and a monologue is by no means the only arbiter of this—the monologue helps us decide if we like you as a person, if you're someone we want to work with, study with, teach, and hire.

The monologue is, then, a reflection of you. What do you want us to know about you? This is why not every monologue works for every actor. Choose carefully. If it doesn't feel right, it most likely isn't. If you think it's a possibility, commit to the piece, do all of the work you can on it, and then perform it for people whose opinions you trust—not just people who tell you everything you do is wonderful (as nice as it is to have those people around). Ask someone who can be honest and helpfully critical.

Our first impulse is to ask, "Did you like it? How was I?"

Unfortunately, "like" is subjective. I can *not* like something yet still be affected by it. Instead, ask questions such as the following: "What did you learn about me from that? What do you think it says about who I am? What was the story? Could you tell what my objective was? Who was I? Did I take you on a journey? Was it playing on different levels, or did it seem too one-note?"

Then take it to a more businesslike level from there: "What am I selling? Does it play to my strengths? What weaknesses are on display in this piece? Does it seem 'type'-appropriate? Did I display a sense of strength as well as vulnerability?"

I will discuss some of these issues further in the pages that follow. However, it's important for an actor of any age to realize that you are selling yourself, and so you need to think like a businessperson. Play to your strengths and overcome your weaknesses. And if you can't overcome your weaknesses, learn how to cover them up! For example, if you can't cry on cue, don't pick a piece that requires you to do so. If you're terrible at telling jokes, don't end your monologue on a punch line.

So, you're a storyteller, an interpreter, and a businessperson. I told you acting was hard work. Pursue this career with an open heart and a tough skin, because for all the applause you'll receive, you'll also receive a lot of criticism and rejection. You have no control over *why* you did or didn't get cast. You do have control over your performance in the room. Focus on telling the story, a story you connect deeply to, and that's a safe and sure foundation.

Now let's begin.

Why Monologues?

Monologues give us a sense of your skill level and your personality.

As a professional casting director, I can think of only two instances in which I've asked actors to prepare a monologue for an audition. The first was when casting the Broadway production of Andrew Lloyd Webber's musical *The Woman in White*, directed by Trevor Nunn. All the actors coming into the room, whether auditioning for a leading role or a place in the ensemble, were asked to prepare music from the show, a contrasting song of their choice, and a Shakespearean monologue. Mr. Nunn, a Shakespearean expert, used the monologue as a way to get to know the actors, direct them, and gauge their ability to handle language and to play objectives and actions. I received a number of calls from agents, managers, and actors saying that they were uncomfortable with Shakespeare and maybe they shouldn't come in. However, I assured them this was the way Mr. Nunn worked, and he wouldn't be judging the actors' ability to handle the language requirements of Shakespeare but rather their ability to tell a story and take direction.

The second instance was when casting the Broadway revival of *Cyrano de Bergerac*. David Leveaux, the director, asked the men coming in for smaller roles, such as the poets and the soldiers, to prepare a classical monologue. In this instance, casting *was* dependent on the actors' ability to handle classical language. We were also able to assign understudy roles from these auditions because, based on the actors' monologue choice, we had a sense of who they were and of their technical and emotional abilities.

Now, that's two instances of using monologues in a more than fifteen-year career in casting. Truth to tell, I don't like monologue auditions. Although they give me a sense of who you are, they don't tell me if you can really act. I know some great actors who are terrible with monologues, and vice versa. Real acting is about collaboration. The true test of an actor is how they perform when faced with a director, another cast member, scenic and lighting elements, props, et cetera. You can be a brilliant performer when on your own and completely crash and burn when faced with a partner to whom you need to be open and receptive.

Nonetheless, as a college professor, I've learned that monologues are very important. Actors use them to audition for a program; we use them for season auditions within the department; and most importantly, my graduating seniors are asked to perform their monologues when they meet with agents and managers after their showcase.

Why? For all the reasons I've previously stated: Do you have the ability to speak with confidence and clarity? Do you have the ability to create a two-minute storytelling and emotional arc? Are you comfortable in your body? Can you play an objective? Can you play an action? Are you in control of your emotional life? Are you someone I want to spend time and work with? A monologue lets us know *who you are*. So it's important that you *know* who you are. And you don't have to be *one* thing, but again, know your strengths.

There appears to be an unwritten rule in schools that urges people away from "storytelling" monologues. In my experience, though, people are at their most active, engaged, and emotionally connected when they are sharing a personal experience. In this book you will find storytelling monologues for this very reason. What you must keep in mind in the performing of them is that we tell stories for a reason. Through these stories, the characters are trying to tell us something about themselves. Therefore, you're telling us something about *you* when you perform it. It's up to you to decide what that is, but make certain you feel emotionally connected to the piece and that you keep it active and engaged with a clear objective.

Now, in the monologues that don't necessarily contain an obvious "story," what do I mean by "storytelling"? I mean you are giving us a brief glimpse into the larger story of that character. You are living out the experience of—bringing to life—a very specific instance in the life of that character. Your plotting of that experience still needs to have a beginning, middle, and end. You must chart your emotional arc for these pieces just as you would if it were a traditional story. Take us on a journey, just the same.

CAUTION: Try not to beat us over the head by living in one extreme emotion for two minutes and simply playing one tactic the entire time. If you do this, your monologue will become monotonous and we will stop listening. Inexperienced actors sometimes think that simply crying or yelling or any generalized emoting is acting. If the character is still talking, it means they haven't achieved their objective yet. And if they haven't achieved their objective yet, it means that they haven't exhausted their arsenal of tactics yet. And if they haven't, you haven't.

Choosing a Monologue

I hope you've come to this book as a starting point. The best way to choose a monologue is to read plays. Read lots and lots of plays. Read every play you can get your hands on. Watch movies and television shows. Searching for—and preparing—monologues requires lots of work. Also, it's your job.

Why should you do all this work? The reasons are plenty, but let me expound upon a few of them.

1. Playwrights are the reason we, as theater professionals, exist. It is our job to honor their work while bringing it to life. You will soon find yourself gravitating to a certain writer or writers. You will want to perform their work. You will seek out productions of theirs wherever you are in the country or the world. You will, eventually, want to work with this playwright and help create new work or revive previous work. You will want to interpret and tell their stories. And—if you move to a city like New York, Los Angeles, or Chicago—you will most likely come into contact with them at some point in time and you can speak with them about their work with knowledge and breadth.

   Conversely, there will be writers you find you don't connect with at all. If this is the case, do not use monologues from their work. You need to love the piece on some very basic level. So even if you can't define why you're not a fan, move on. Pick up the play a few months or years later and read it again. Maybe you'll come at it from a different perspective and it will connect with you. It may never.

   Finally, many of these playwrights you love and admire get hired to write, produce, and run television shows. Whether in New York or L.A., you will come across a writer who has moved from theater to the film industry for any number of reasons (money). You will find, I bet, their heart still remains in the theater, and they will love to hear you are a fan of theirs.

2. You'll come across monologues that aren't right for you at this point in your life but can be put on the shelf and pulled out again when you're in your late twenties, early thirties, forties, or even sixties. Yes, people in their fifties and sixties still audition, no matter who or where they are. The work, if you're lucky, never ends.

3. When you read these plays and watch TV shows and films, you're researching. You're finding out which actors are getting cast in the parts you want to play. Follow their careers. This is how you begin to track and define your "type." This is how you learn what parts are out there for you. The cast list that precedes the play in most published work is a guide for you. Google the actors and find out who they are and what they've done.

The actress Saidah Arrika Ekulona (you don't know who she is? Google her. It's your job) spoke to my students recently and said, "Don't worry about so much about your type. Don't obsess about it. Somebody, somewhere is ready to put you in a box, so why should you do it for yourself?" I wholeheartedly agree—and disagree—with her! Here's where I agree: of course you must believe you can do anything, play any part. You need to constantly raise the bar for yourself so that you have goals to work toward. Just because you're the "ingénue" or "the leading man" doesn't mean you can't also find the humor, sexuality, and hunger in those roles. You need to find the complexities and polarities in every role you play. People are complicated, and therefore so are characters.

However, you also need to keep in mind that this is a business. And people in business want to know how you're marketable. So if you have a list of actors who are doing the things you know how to do, playing the parts you know you can play, you are armed with information that's going to help you market yourself. Don't think of defining your type as a "box." It's not. It's a marketing strategy.

It may sound like a cliché, but knowledge is power. And your knowledge of these plays, writers, and fellow actors is your weapon. Put it to use.

4. Films and TV are fair game when searching for material. However, you want to stay away from material that would be considered "iconic." Avoid characters that are firmly ingrained in our popular culture. Shows like *Girls*, *Sex and the City*, or *Friends* have great writing, but that writing became more and more tailored to the specific actors playing those roles as the seasons progressed. It is difficult to approach that material without hearing the voices of those original actors in our heads. So enjoy those shows, but don't use them, even if your type is a Carrie, a Charlotte, a Joey, or a Chandler.

5. Sometimes you'll find a character that you really like but who doesn't have a stand-alone monologue in the play. You'll be tempted to cut and paste the lines together until you form it into something that seems complete. I caution you away from this. Although some of the pieces in this

book have been edited, there has been no major cutting and rearranging. I find that it destroys the author's intent. You're crafting a piece into something it wasn't meant to be. Look at something else by this writer. Or search for a similar character in another play. Your "type" work will come in handy here. The actor who played this role was also in what other plays? This writer has also written what other plays?

6. Once you've chosen a monologue from this book (or from a play or film), please read the entire work. Then read it again. Then—read it again. Although you will ultimately be performing the piece out of context, you can act it well only if you can make sense of the context in which it was written.

Preparing the Monologue

I am asking you to do a lot of work here. But if this monologue leads to landing a job or an agent or gets you into the grad school of your choice, then you want to do as much preparation as possible to make it a complete, worthwhile experience for you and the people behind the table.

I've heard from many actors over the years that they don't want to be "over-rehearsed." They want to keep their piece "fresh." If you feel your piece is over-rehearsed, then you are doing something wrong. There is no such thing. The amount of work that goes into keeping a piece fresh and alive is endless. Ask someone who has been in a Broadway show for six months, or a year. There is always something more to unearth in a role, especially if you keep clarifying and refining your objective, actions, and relationships.

Here's how to start.

1. Read the entire play.
2. Read the entire play again.
3. Read it one more time.
4. Although you will have been very tempted to do so, do *not* read the monologue out loud yet. You've read the play a few times now, and you're beginning to, consciously or unconsciously, realize the intention of the piece in the whole.
5. Have a notebook handy to write down your initial thoughts, reactions, and responses to the play, the characters, and the relationships.

I want you to think about the play as a whole, first, by asking these questions:

Is this a dramatic or a comedic monologue?

This is a tough question. I find that most good monologues walk the line between the two, putting them in the "seriocomic" category. A comedic monologue is not always about landing a joke. A comedic monologue shows that you can handle material that is light and playful while still playing a strong objective and having an emotional connection to the text. A dramatic monologue tackles more serious issues, events, and emotions. Be careful that your dramatic monologue doesn't dissolve into you screaming and/or crying in the direction of the auditioner. This is *not* a sign that you can act. If you're crying and screaming, then you are most likely not playing an objective or using strong actions. You're just being self-indulgent.

In life, we rarely get what we want when we scream or cry at people. It's no different in acting.

What are some of the major themes of the play?

It is often easiest to define your character's objective by wording it to include the main themes or images in the play.

Themes are the major ideas or topics of the play, together with the writer's point of view on these topics. Sometimes the theme will reveal itself through repetition of imagery, such as the sun and flight imagery I mentioned earlier in *Romeo and Juliet*.

Make a list of these themes, both major and minor, in your notebook.

What does the title of the play mean?

The author's intention or point of view is often most clearly defined in the title of the play. Thinking about it might also lead you to define the main theme of the work, as just discussed. Your work on the theme of the play should lead you directly here.

Who is the main character in the play?

Whose story is it? What is their journey? If you're performing a monologue of the main character, how does the piece affect their progression? If you're performing a piece from a supporting character, how does it assist or impede the main character's journey?

The main character is the person who takes the biggest journey over the course of the play. Your monologue is one of the following: (1) the person on that journey; (2) a person helping the main character on that journey; (3) a person creating an obstacle to the main character achieving their goal.

Even in an ensemble play, there is always a main character.

What is your objective?

This question is twofold, because I'm asking you to define your objective for both the play and the monologue. You need to define what this character wants throughout the entire play—from the moment he or she steps onto the stage. Then you need to define how this two-minute (or so) piece fits into the whole.

An objective is a *simple*, *active*, *positive* statement that defines the journey your character is on.

It is in defining an objective that most young actors tend to hinder their performance. You never want to define your objective in the following ways: (1) I want "to *be* something," or (2) I want "to *feel* something." These are passive, inactive statements in which you will not make any forward progression. Emotion does play a role in acting, but not when it comes to defining an objective.

Instead I want you to define it in very vivid, active words that inspire you and spark your imagination. This is where your knowledge of the entire play and the character you are creating comes into action.

Begin by thinking in very primal terms. Objectives should hold life-or-death stakes: companionship, shelter, protection, nourishment, sex, fight, and flight.

"I want to hold my family together" is a very strong objective.

"I want to make someone love me" is another.

However, I challenge you to take it a step further. If you're working on Kirsten Greenidge's *Milk Like Sugar*, you might start with "I want to create a better life for myself." But you can use the language and the imagery from the play, taking your objective into deeper territory: "I want to taste the sweetest, most expensive milk I can find." The more vividly you can paint the objective, especially by using words and images from the play itself, the better.

Play your objective with the belief that you're going to WIN! Play positive choices. We don't go to the theater to see people lose. We want to see them try to overcome. Even if they don't succeed. If you start acting with the knowledge that you're going to lose, what's the point of telling the story?

I can't stress enough that every time you step in front of someone to act, you must have an objective. Every time. Whether you're performing a monologue, a song, or an entire play, you must have an objective. It's one of the basic conditions of acting. If you don't have an objective, you don't have a goal, and there's no reason to act (or to watch). Even if you find out that objective doesn't work, commit to it while you're performing and then try something else the next time.

I have asked many an actor in an audition what their objective was only to get silence in return. Not every casting director is going to do this and then give you another chance. Figure out what you want to *do* before you come into the room. Otherwise, you're wasting your time and ours.

What are the beats and actions?

A *beat* is a transition: a change in thought, action, subject, or tactic.

Not every line is a new beat. Try to find it organically. When it feels like there is a shift in thought, there most likely is. That is your beat. Trust your instincts. Are you accomplishing what you want? Are you winning? If not, it's time to shift your tactic.

Have you been playing the same tactic over and over without achieving your goal? It's time to shift your tactic. Backtrack: when did that start? How can you adjust?

Actions are active verbs that define what you are doing in any particular moment. Meaning, you attach an active verb to every line of text: to sway, to punish, to defend, to challenge, and so on.

Actions become your roadmap, your markers. If you're a musician, think of them as musical notes. The note is written there, but it's up to you to color it, make it your own, and endow it with meaning. Engage your own unique point of view to make it personal. However, every new action does not necessarily mean you've come to a beat change. Again, feel it out instinctively. You should have an action for every line. Hard work, I know. However, this work makes you really pay attention to the language of the play and the words you are using to achieve your objective.

You cannot consciously play these objectives, beats, actions, and tactics, but you must rehearse with them in mind so that you can internalize them. Once they've become internalized, they will play themselves. It's a form of muscle memory. The challenge then becomes to trust that the work is there and let it go.

Check in with your (imaginary) scene partner. Make sure your actions are landing. This is where your imagination comes into play. When you look at the empty space you have to see how they're reacting, how they're looking (or not looking) at you.

Playing actions helps in two areas: it helps you do more than play the "mood" of the piece. Mood is established in the arc of the storytelling, not in the way you say the lines. Mood is also established in how you're relating to the other person: are you winning, or losing? Secondly, playing actions will help you not play the end of the monologue at the beginning. If the monologue ends in death, you don't want us to know that when you start. Take us there without letting us know we're going to get there.

When I was working as the assistant director of Martin Mc-Donagh's Broadway production of *A Behanding in Spokane*, John Crowley, the director, would sit at the table with the actors every afternoon after lunch and make them assign actions to every line of text. We did this for weeks. It is oftentimes very frustrating, but it lets you know where you're going. It forces you into specificity. And if any particular action doesn't seem to work for you, throw it out and try another! That is why actors rehearse.

Right now you're asking yourself why you need to do all of this work. Let's go back to the words that opened this book: Actors are storytellers, and the best stories are those told with specificity. Think of this monologue as a smaller story inside a larger one. You need to understand the larger story the playwright is telling in order to tell this shorter story. You need to know the details in order to bring them to life.

The greater your understanding of the piece as a whole, the better your ability to interpret it. Doing all of this work doesn't take all the fun out of performing. The more information we have, the deeper we can go and the more fun we can have. Specificity leads to freedom.

Remember, people rarely expect to speak in monologue form. Have an expectation of how you think your (unseen) partner may react. This is part of a conversation, and your partner is letting you speak for quite a bit of time, or you are not letting them get a word in. Don't approach it as a monologue; approach it as dialogue. Expect your scene partner to cut you off. Your expectation is key to why you go on for some two minutes. Pay attention to and play with your partner. Oftentimes this expectation of interruption will help you bring a sense of urgency to the piece.

Inevitably, you will be performing these monologues for someone who knows the play. You want your acting of the monologue to be consistent with the tone, theme, and style of the play, as well as the character's objective within it. You can't take a monologue from *Macbeth*, for example, and mine it for high comic potential. You'll look foolish, and the casting director will assume you don't know what you're doing.

Who is your character?

Once you've answered all of the above questions, it's time to start putting this person into your body.

1. What do they look like?
2. How do they dress?
3. How do they stand?
4. Where is their center of gravity?
5. How do they take up space?
6. What's their posture?
7. Where does their voice sit (i.e., head, throat, chest, diaphragm, etc.)?
8. Where do they hold tension?
9. How do they walk, sit, and stand?

It's up to you to find this person in your body—experiment with them. Holding on to what you know about them from the script, and your very strong objective, you'll be able to find physicality for them through your knowledge of them.

If you can imagine them, you can become them.

Whom is your character talking to?

These are monologues, but you need to have a very specific picture of *whom* you are talking to, because it plays directly into *why* you are talking (your objective). Some of these monologues are to a specific person, or persons; some were written as audience address. You still need to decide to whom, specifically, it is directed and have a clear image of that person.

Place that person somewhere in the room with you. You should never perform your monologue directly to the person for whom you are auditioning unless they ask. You can place them, in your imagination, to the left or the right and a little in front of that person. You can place them behind that person and a little above their head. You can place them closer to you, to your immediate left, right, or center. However, make sure that they're not so close that you are forced to look down while you deliver your monologue. We need to see your face.

Now that you've placed your "acting partner" somewhere, you need to imagine what they look like.

1. What are they wearing?
2. Are they sitting, or standing?
3. What is your relationship to them?
4. What do you need from them? (This ties in to your objective)
5. How is delivering this monologue bringing you closer to achieving your goal?
6. By the end of the monologue, did you win? Did you get what you wanted? Are you closer or further away from achieving you goal?

If you can imagine them vividly and specifically, we will see them.

What's so urgent?

Younger actors often lack a sense of urgency. Remember, your character is dealing with life-and-death stakes! Urgent doesn't mean "do it quickly." Urgent means: why do you need to say these things right now? Why do you need to achieve your objective right now? What just happened that makes every word in this monologue so important? This should carry life-or-death stakes: *If I don't achieve this objective right now, my life will fall apart.*

Using the language to your advantage (covered in a section that follows) will guarantee that you can add heat to your monologue without rushing through.

The quality of your time on stage is much more important than the quantity. Please don't think that the longer you take, the more illustrative you're being.

Emotional Connection

Up until now I have hardly mentioned feelings, emotions, or emoting. You must, of course, have a strong emotional connection to the monologue you choose. Your connection may grow or dissipate when you complete the work outlined above. Sometimes the more you discover about a play, or a character, the further it feels from your initial response. If this is the case, and you can't reclaim that initial spark, then move on to something else. You can always find another piece.

Conversely, your initial response to the monologue might be only so-so until you do more work on it, finding yourself truly enlivened and engaged by it. In that case, take it and run.

Acting is not about emoting. Young actors tend to find pieces with very high emotional stakes that often require crying or screaming in order to accomplish the storytelling. Please shy away from these. We want to see that you are emotionally connected to the material and that you know how to *control* your emotional life. We do not want to have your emotions unleashed upon us in a flood that you cannot contain. Therefore, a monologue that occurs at the climax of a play is probably best left performed in the context of the show.

After performing all of the work laid about above, your emotional connection to the piece should be growing organically. You relationship to the character, his/her objective, the relationships, and the story should be incredibly strong. You should find yourself invested in living through the experience and sharing the story.

If you feel that you are still generating (read: *forcing*) an emotional reaction in order to make the monologue work for you, I would suggest putting it aside. You don't want us to see you working hard in order to put the material over.

Language and Point of View

I've talked a lot about your relationship to language and how you need to have one. Words and punctuation, as provided by the writer, can sometimes unlock the key to your character. Language is how these characters express what they need. Please use the words to your advantage.

Nothing about the language is secondary. If there weren't words, there wouldn't be a story.

Remember that acting occurs *on* the lines, not in between them. Try to express what you're feeling by coloring a word or a phrase with your point of view while maintaining the flow of the line. Tie your thoughts together without breaking the line apart in pieces in an attempt to highlight certain words.

The line is your thought and your action: present it completely. Try not to add moments, beats, unexpressed thoughts, and feelings in between the lines. It's not necessary. Use what the playwright has given you.

If the playwright wants you to take time somewhere, they will provide the clues. It can be as specific as them writing *pause* or *beat*.

There are other clues, though:

An ellipsis (...) often signifies a trailing off of thought or a search for the right thing to say.

A hyphen or dash (—) often signifies a break in thought, a cut-off thought, or a new idea.

These are basically the only times you have permission to break up the thought. Otherwise, see your energy through the entire line. Stay engaged and alive, and keep the thought moving.

A word or a line written in all caps means the author wants you to highlight that particular section, but it does not necessarily mean you need to yell and scream it.

Be aware of repetition. If a writer uses the same word or phrase repeatedly, they're trying to tell you something. How you shade that word (or don't) each time it comes up says something about the character and what they're after.

Also, pay attention to periods, question marks, exclamation points, and other basic punctuation marks. These are not arbitrary. Something delivered as a statement has a completely different meaning if it's intended to be delivered as a question. This isn't your decision to make if the writer has shown otherwise.

If you're working on an Adam Bock piece (*Swimming in the Shallows* in this book, for example), you'll notice a suspicious lack of punctuation. He is specifically writing characters searching for their point of view, unable to make decisions, living in a world of ambivalence. You need to commit to each of these thoughts, but he's leaving it up to you to figure out what each could be.

Point of view is how you (your character) see the world, relate to the people and objects around you, and relate to language. This is where artistry occurs. Anyone can say the words. How you give them meaning, how you filter all of this through your perspective, is what makes your interpretation unique.

Also what is your point of view on the person to whom you're speaking? This has to go deeper than "I like him" or "I don't like her." Who is she to you? "My sister," for example, is a surface definition. "This is the one person in the world I've shared all my secrets with my entire life" takes it a step further. "This is the one person in the world I've shared all my secrets with in my entire life, but she's never had her heart broken and doesn't understand how I'm feeling" takes it even further. More importantly, can this person help you achieve your objective, or are they standing in your way?

Your point of view must be apparent when you talk about a person or a place that has an emotional effect on you: your mother, your father, your sister, or your brother. Or you could be speaking about your childhood home or your favorite restaurant. How do you feel about them? Where in your body do you feel them when you speak about them?

Point of view is what makes the character *yours*.

Edit

You can't have everything. You can't make every moment last a lifetime. All of the tools I've provided you with are an effort to keep you active and engaged and in the moment. If you find yourself lingering over a word, a phrase, a pause, I want you to ask yourself *why*. Is it necessary? Are you staying true to the storytelling, the author's intention, and the character's objective? Will hanging out in that moment help you achieve your objective faster, better, with more urgency? Will screaming, crying, and wailing do the same? In both cases, probably not.

Finally, it's time for you to put all of the pieces together. You have all the elements of the story, and now you need to get from point A, to point B, to point C. This takes a long rehearsal process. It means experimenting with all of these elements. If something does not work, throw it away and try something else. If something seems to maybe, kind of work, hold on to it and experiment inside of that. Try doing the entire piece in a whisper and see what you learn. Try doing it at the top of your voice in a public place and see what you discover. Take risks with how you rehearse it and you might find something you never knew was there.

I strongly urge you *not* to practice these monologues in front of a mirror. It will only make you feel self-conscious, and you will put your focus and energy into how you look while you do it rather than into what you are *doing*. Instead, practice it in front of friends and family. Practice achieving your objective on them. Practice your actions on them.

You have created a roadmap, but that doesn't mean you can't take side trips. Your objective is in mind; now try a roundabout way of getting there. Remember, these are called "plays," and you should, in fact, play. Have fun.

In Performance

You are ready to perform the monologue in public. Here are a few quick tips for the audition room:

Some actors think it doesn't matter how they present themselves when they enter or exit the audition room. Your audition starts the moment the door opens and doesn't end until you leave.

1. Arrive early. At least fifteen minutes before your appointment time. You need this time to unclutter your mind, focus yourself, and relax.

2. When your name is called, close your eyes and take a deep breath in and out. Find your center.

3. Take as few of your personal items into the room as necessary. Try not to bring in your jacket, your bag, your purse, your gym clothes, and so on. Gentlemen, please take phones, keys, and loose change out of your front pockets; do not interrupt the natural line of your body.

4. Say a friendly "Hello" to the person or persons in the room, even if they seem engaged in another activity. Very often, we are writing notes about whoever just exited, but we will try to make contact and greet you, the next person entering the room, especially to see if you look like your headshot.

5. Look like your headshot.

6. Leave your bitterness, your disappointment, and your desperation outside of the door. There's no room for it in the audition.

We can sense all of them. If you put your energy into your emotions instead of into telling the story, you will not get cast. This is a business, like any other, filled with unfairness and disappointments. Don't take it out on the people behind the table. Don't sabotage yourself. The only thing that matters is the work. You can bitch to your friends later. But we can sense your negativity, and we don't want it.

7. Do not advance on the table, introduce yourself, and attempt to shake hands. Keep a friendly, professional distance unless the person behind the table makes a move otherwise. We sometimes see a hundred people in one day; we can't shake everyone's hand.

8. Be nice to everyone in the room, including the reader and the accompanist. We take note of that. Remember we're looking to form an ensemble, and how you treat everyone matters. Also remember that today's accompanist is tomorrow's up-and-coming composer.

9. Do not apologize for what you're about to do or explain that you:

    a. Are sick.

    b. Have just been sick.

    c. Feel as if you're getting sick.

10. Find a comfortable space to stand, or ask for a chair if you're using one. There will almost always be a chair available for you. It makes no difference to us whether you stand or sit, but it sometimes makes a difference to your monologue.

11. Once you're in position, please introduce yourself and let us know the title of the play from which the monologue comes.

12. Take a moment before you begin. Close your eyes or turn away from us. Center yourself. Runners don't hit the track and begin running. They take their position, they focus themselves, they wait for the gun, and then they go. In this situation, you are in charge of the gun. The room is yours when you walk in. As you arrived some fifteen minutes before entering the room, this shouldn't take more than a second or two. Please, no slumping in place, no shaking out your arms and legs, no vocalizing. All of this should be done at home or outside the room. The moment before is simply to focus.

13. Act! Have fun. We want you to be good. We want to welcome you into our program, our school, and our cast. Worry less about getting it "right" and concentrate on telling us a story.

13a. Sometimes you start off on the wrong foot. That's okay. You can stop and ask if you can start again. Take a breath. Focus. Start again. If it doesn't happen the second time, you should kindly apologize and leave the room. You're not prepared. You've not done enough work on the piece, or you're letting your nerves get the better of you. There are no tried-and-true tricks for beating this. Comfort and familiarity with the material, combined with a desire to tell the story, are your best bets!

14. Keep it to two minutes. All of the monologues in this book fulfill that requirement, and some are shorter. You do not need to use the entire two minutes. We can very often tell if we're interested in someone within the first thirty seconds to a minute.

15. When you've finished, take a beat and end the piece. Give us a cue that your performance is over and you're no longer the character. Again, be careful of judging your work while in the room. I've seen many actors want to apologize or make a face that says, "Well, that didn't go the way I had planned it." Whether it was your best work or your worst work, don't let us know.

16. There's a fine line between lingering and rushing out of the room. Sometimes we may ask you a question or two in an effort to get to know you better. Stay focused and centered until we say, "Thank you."

17. Your résumé should be a reflection of your work. Please don't lie on it in any way, shape, or form! Don't say you've worked with people or on productions that you never have! If you were in the ensemble, don't say you were the lead! We've all been in the ensemble. It's okay.

18. Enjoy telling the story.

In this book I'm providing you with a summary of the play, a brief character description, and a list of questions you should ask yourself when approaching the material. However, I urge you to seek out the play and read it in its entirety so that you can have a greater understanding of the character, the situations, and the events.

Most importantly, when performing any of these pieces, play a strong, simple, vivid objective; maintain a deep emotional connection to the material; act on the line; have a sense of urgency; and know why, and to whom, you're speaking.

Some of the monologues included in this volume are very short. I find it's helpful to have these in your back pocket in case you are asked to do something else and want something quick that packs a punch. As I said earlier, you can provide a good sense of what you can do in a relatively short amount of time.

Conversely, some of these pieces are long. I am providing you with alternate cuts within the larger structure that, I believe, maintain the original intent of the author and still provide storytelling opportunities.

Etiquette for Scene Study, Rehearsal, and Beyond

My recent experiences as a college professor and associate director led me to discover that some of the things I assumed were obvious (in regards to behavior, attitude, and work ethic) for actors of all ages and levels were, in fact, not.

The second you walk in the door, you are there to serve the work, not your ego.

No matter who you are in the show, you are part of an ensemble, and every move you make affects that. The ensemble extends to everyone working on the production: stage management, director, crew, stage door man, et cetera. Each of these people deserves your attention and respect.

I compiled this list in response to that discovery and have a feeling it will keep evolving over my lifetime and, hopefully, beyond. It might not necessarily serve you in an audition setting, but keep it in mind once you book the job.

First-Day-of-Rehearsal Behavior

- Be present. Everyone is nervous and excited.
- Do not isolate yourself.
- Approach individuals and introduce yourself.
- Tell them what your role is (even if you're an understudy).
- Make conversation by asking questions.

- Seek out the director, producer, and casting director and thank them for the opportunity.
- During the read-through, don't highlight your lines. *Listen* to the play.
- During the read-through, don't look ahead to see when you're next on stage. *Listen* to the play.

First Read-through and Every Rehearsal

- Dress appropriately
  - ° Dress in a silhouette similar to your character. If your character wears long pants, do not rehearse in shorts. If your character wears a skirt, wear a skirt.
  - ° Do not wear clothing with logos or slogans printed on it. You want your partner focusing on you, your face, your body, and your behavior, *not* reading your T-shirt or laughing at the funny print on it.
  - ° Do not wear open-toed shoes or sandals ever, unless the role requires them. Do not rehearse a fight scene in these shoes *ever*.
  - ° Do not change your hair length, color, or style at any time before rehearsal starts or during the process without consulting your director first.
- Practice Personal Hygiene
  - ° Brush your teeth before every rehearsal and after every break, especially after eating or smoking.
  - ° Shower every day and before every performance.

- ○ Wear clean clothes to rehearsal every day. If you wear the same things, figure out a way to wash them as much as possible.
- ○ Go to the gym. Eight shows a week require strength and stamina. Film shoots can be long and exhausting.
- ○ If you go to the gym before rehearsal, shower.
- ○ Get seven to eight hours of sleep a night.
- ○ Drink and smoke in moderation.
- Bring a pencil and paper with you. Every day. Have backups.
- Phones are not a place to take notes at any time during the process.
- Character idea: Have one based on an intelligent reading and analysis of the script.
- Your character idea should be flexible. The director may steer you in a different direction. Try it for a few days. If it doesn't feel right, explain this and use your reading and analysis of the script to support your case. Ultimately, your director has the final say.
- Don't emphasize pronouns and verbs. These are very often the least interesting words in the sentence.
- Don't be late. Give yourself time to arrive at least ten minutes early. You should be ready to work at start time, not arriving. If you need time to warm up, factor this into your travel time.
- *Listen.* Listen to everyone.
- Pay attention to what the director says about the world of the play. Even if it does not immediately give you information

about your character specifically, he or she is sharing their vision of the show with you. You can very often pick up something valuable to use immediately or in the future as you create your character. This information informs your choices.

- Don't ask too many questions right away. Don't make everything about your character and you. The rehearsal process is one of discovery, and you shouldn't discover everything in the first week. Also, if you *listen*, you may discover the answers to your questions without having to ask.

- Look up the definition and pronunciation of any unfamiliar word or reference.

- Find an activity for every scene you're in. We rarely sit and talk. Activity creates behavior. This activity should be rooted in the text and what the text says you could or should be doing.

- Don't confuse your *fear* with your *process*. It is your job to take risks in rehearsal, and this doesn't always happen in your comfort zone or when you are ready to. *Jump* when the director asks you to without asking "How high?" first.

- Don't use the word "process" to defend your insecurities. The director has a process, too, and that's to get a performance out of you, and it doesn't always happen on your terms. Your "process" is not an excuse to not try something the director is asking.

- Unless otherwise instructed, be off-book the second time you get to a scene.

- Use the rehearsal room as your opportunity to *take chances*.

- Don't stand in your own way. Listen to the script and your director, not your ego.
- Don't enter a scene to "have a scene" with your partner. It's your job to keep that person in the room, and vice versa. You're coming in to achieve something, and the other person is either going to help or hinder you. Live truthfully within that knowledge.
- Always find a sense of urgency in your character.
- Always find a sense of humor in your character.

Men's Monologues

Tabletop
Rob Ackerman

JEFFREY

You are such a putz. In every way.

We're not messengers, Ron, we're snake oil salesmen. We are creating needs, not satisfying them. We're helping Americans grow increasingly obese, bringing them new sorts of artificial sweeteners, new kinds of carcinogens, new pieces of unnecessary plastic. If something is actually good for you, Ron, it doesn't get a television commercial. When was the last time you saw a spot for organic asparagus? But we'll happily dedicate billions of dollars and hours to snack cakes and fizzy beverages. We corrupt the children, depress the adults and destroy the last dregs of independent thinking.

That is our profession, Ron. That is what they're paying us for.

Analysis: *Tabletop*

Type: Comic
Synopsis

Rob Ackerman's biting comedy explores hierarchy and tensions in the workplace. This particular workplace is a Manhattan studio set up for filming television commercials. Everyone who works here has a specific, union-protected job. Work is done quickly and efficiently without much creativity or thought. It's a factory. No one oversteps the boundaries of their specific duties—except for Ron. Ron is relatively new, inexperienced, and eager. He wants to prove himself, he wants to get ahead, and he wants to show off his creativity. He does all of this with a surprising lack of arrogance.

Jeffrey, on the other hand, is more seasoned. He does all he can to keep Ron in his place. Today the company is filming two commercials: one for a "thick pink" liquid that gets poured over fruit and the other for a new ice cream–like treat for a fast-food company. All of this happens under the maniacal, controlling hand of their boss, Marcus. Marcus rules with an iron fist, threatening and belittling his staff. The fear he instills in his employees keeps everyone in place, doing *only* the jobs they are hired for, no more, no less.

Ron comes up with alternate ways to achieve effects in the thirty-second spots, but he fails at their execution. Jeffrey loves this because it gives him the opportunity to pull rank and school his inexperienced colleague on how things work. Marcus finally fires Ron, in a spectacular tirade. He also loses the respect of all his employees. Ron retaliates with such ferocity that everyone on staff stands up to the bully boss.

Character Description
Jeffrey, 30s
The on-set property master. He is a cocky professional craftsperson. His daily wardrobe consists of jeans, a polo, and a pair of New

Balance sneakers. He is constantly putting Ron in place—whether out of insecurity or downright mean-spiritedness is up to you to decide. He calls it "teasing," but it reads as disrespect. Whereas Ron sees himself and the other staff as artisans, Jeffrey thinks of them as technicians. He says, "We're supposed to just do it, okay? We implement. We do not invent. We're limbs, okay? Arms and fingers, not hearts and minds." This point of view tells you almost everything you need to know about him. This point of view also makes him Marcus's "favorite son." Marcus never takes his anger or aggression out on Jeffrey, because Jeffrey follows and implements the rules. He plays the game better than anyone there.

Over the course of the play, Jeffrey takes credit for the "swirl" Ron creates for the fast-food company. He also learns a few tricks from the younger employee. But he never shows his appreciation. If anything, they only serve to fuel his dislike for Ron. Jeffrey likes everything in place, ordered and structured. Ron's upstart ways only serve to knock them continually off balance.

Given Circumstances

Who are they? Ron is the younger, less experienced co-worker of Jeffrey, the seasoned professional.

Where are they? On the set of a television commercial working under a strict time constraint.

When does this take place? On a Monday in the present.

Why are they there? They are filming a commercial for a thick pink fruit-based liquid.

What is the pre-beat? Ron has just waxed poetic about how they are Renaissance men and inventors, whose job is to make people enjoy their lives.

Questions

1. What does a property master do?
2. How long has Jeffrey been doing this?
3. How did he get here?
4. What did he set out to be?
5. What is the difference between an artisan and a technician?
6. What does Jeffrey like about his job?
7. Does he really like/respect Marcus?
8. What is it about Ron's idealism that rubs Jeffrey wrong?
9. What does Ron look like?
10. Why does Jeffrey feel it's necessary to pull rank/school Ron?
11. Why does he take credit for Ron's "swirl"?
12. This is a high-pressure job. How does Jeffrey function under pressure?
13. How does Jeffrey relax? What does he do in his downtime?
14. What's the difference between Jeffrey at home and Jeffrey at work?
15. What do order and control mean to Jeffrey? Conversely, what does chaos mean to him?

Tabletop
Rob Ackerman

JEFFREY

Artists are food. Okay? They come in here and fag around for a few minutes with their fabric swatches and flower arrangements and then they're chewed up and shat out. Artists are plankton; Marcus is the whale. Listen, Ron, you want to hear how it works?

This liquid, this luscious stream of liquid, is what it's all about. And there's this corporation with these stockholders and this board of directors. And they're gonna start making a lot of money off this liquid. And sales will create jobs. And jobs will create sales. And this liquid is like *blood* and we're here at the *aorta* of capitalism, okay? And all that blood is rushing right by. And it's rich. And it's oxygenated. And we can't spill a drop. If we can manage to not spill a drop, we get to stick around and drink, don't we? But only if we don't fuck up. That's all that really matters. Not fucking up.

Analysis: *Tabletop*

Type: Comic
Synopsis

Rob Ackerman's biting comedy explores hierarchy and tensions
in the workplace. This particular workplace is a Manhattan studio
set up for filming television commercials. Everyone who works
here has a specific, union-protected job. Work is done quickly and
efficiently without much creativity or thought. It's a factory. No
one oversteps the boundaries of their specific duties—except for
Ron. Ron is relatively new, inexperienced, and eager. He wants to
prove himself, he wants to get ahead, and he wants to show off his
creativity. He does all of this with a surprising lack of arrogance.

Jeffrey, on the other hand, is more seasoned. He does all he
can to keep Ron in his place. Today the company is filming two
commercials: one for a "thick pink" liquid that gets poured over
fruit and the other for a new ice cream–like treat for a fast-food
company. All of this happens under the maniacal, controlling
hand of their boss, Marcus. Marcus rules with an iron fist, threatening and belittling his staff. The fear he instills in his employees
keeps everyone in place, doing *only* the jobs they are hired for,
no more, no less.

Ron comes up with alternate ways to achieve effects in the
thirty-second spots, but he fails at their execution. Jeffrey loves
this because it gives him the opportunity to pull rank and school
his inexperienced colleague on how things work. Marcus finally
fires Ron, in a spectacular tirade. He also loses the respect of all

his employees. Ron retaliates with such ferocity that everyone on staff stands up to the bully boss.

Character Description
Jeffrey, 30s

The on-set property master. He is a cocky professional craftsperson. His daily wardrobe consists of jeans, a polo, and a pair of New Balance sneakers. He is constantly putting Ron in place—whether out of insecurity or downright mean-spiritedness is up to you to decide. He calls it "teasing," but it reads as disrespect. Whereas Ron sees himself and the other staff as artisans, Jeffrey thinks of them as technicians. He says, "We're supposed to just do it, okay? We implement. We do not invent. We're limbs, okay? Arms and fingers, not hearts and minds." This point of view tells you almost everything you need to know about him. This point of view also makes him Marcus's "favorite son." Marcus never takes his anger or aggression out on Jeffrey, because Jeffrey follows and implements the rules. He plays the game better than anyone there.

Over the course of the play, Jeffrey takes credit for the "swirl" Ron creates for the fast-food company. He also learns a few tricks from the younger employee. But he never shows his appreciation. If anything, they only serve to fuel his dislike for Ron. Jeffrey likes everything in place, ordered and structured. Ron's upstart ways only serve to knock them continually off balance.

Given Circumstances

Who are they? Ron is the younger, less experienced co-worker of Jeffrey, the seasoned professional.

Where are they? On the set of a television commercial working under a strict time constraint.

When does this take place? On a Monday in the present.

Why are they there? They are filming a commercial for a thick pink fruit-based liquid.

What is the pre-beat? The entire team is trying to break Ron's idealism and explain how they're soldiers, not creative professionals.

Questions

1. What does a property master do?
2. How long has Jeffrey been doing this?
3. How did he get here?
4. What did he set out to be?
5. What is the difference between an artisan and a technician?
6. What does Jeffrey like about his job?
7. Does he really like/respect Marcus?
8. What is it about Ron's idealism that rubs Jeffrey wrong?
9. What does Ron look like?
10. Why does Jeffrey feel it's necessary to pull rank/school Ron?
11. Why does he take credit for Ron's "swirl"?
12. This is a high-pressure job. How does Jeffrey function under pressure?
13. How does Jeffrey relax? What does he do in his downtime?
14. What's the difference between Jeffrey at home and Jeffrey at work?
15. What do order and control mean to Jeffrey? Conversely, what does chaos mean to him?

Carol Mulroney
Stephen Belber

KEN

I've always been a huge admirer of sadness; of sad people; of people who don't understand something very . . . vital. We live in a world where sadness is devalued, where sad people are considered . . . incompetent. And maybe we are, for there are many ways to be happy and you'd think that we would just embrace one, but . . .

Carol had sadness running through her veins like bad blood. Consequently, I was drawn to her immediately. I dunno. I just wanna love them; the sad people; people like Carol. I just want to love. Because it's what I'm good at— maybe the only thing I have, this skill of love—this skill *to* love. I love to love. I do. I love it. *(Pause.)* The problem is that the world tends not to love me back. Which makes me very sad. *(Pause.)* And it's a great disappointment because it should; the world, or certain people in it, they *should* love me back. And I get so mad at them when they don't. Because I know I know how to solve them, to help *solve* their sadness. But it's like at some point they just stop listening; like they get too close to the edge . . . and they lose their ability to focus. And I get so angry . . . that this beautiful, sad person standing in front of me can't see how much potential happiness I'm offering them. It's like . . . "Why can't you just be fucking happy?" When of course I already know the answer. Which is that sometimes you just miss the train.

Analysis: *Carol Mulroney*

Type: Dramatic
Synopsis

Carol Mulroney stands on her rooftop looking out over the city, a city she finds "uncompromisingly beautiful." Unfortunately, that beauty is visible only from afar. Up close and inside, it's messy, chaotic, and hurtful. Carol comes to the roof in search of solace and reflection.

She has recently found out that her mother's death was, in fact, a suicide. Already suffering from depression, Carol is pushed even deeper down into it by this discovery. Carol's father, Hutton, runs a major cosmetics corporation. He is powerful and wealthy. Carol's husband, Lesley, works for the company and is up for a promotion. Lesley's co-worker Ken is up for the same job. Hutton has come to Carol to tell her that he is leaning toward promoting Ken over Lesley. Hutton wants to rebuild his relationship with Carol, but she blames him for her mother's suicide.

Carol and Lesley are unhappy. Lesley has always been macho, prone to violence, but he's trying to control that and put his life together. He wants children, but Carol does not. Lesley has been having an affair with their friend Joan.

Ken is in love with Carol. Ken does not want the promotion; he wants to form his own cosmetics company, but he's been saying that for years. Carol drinks a lot, sometimes with her friend Joan, sometimes alone. Occasionally, she paints. Everyone feels stuck.

Carol falls off the roof and dies.

The big question of the play, as posed by Belber, seems to be: who controls our lives? Do we control our own destiny? Are we governed by fate? Do other people's actions affect the course of our lives? Carol blames Hutton for ruining her life, and so she makes every decision based on that belief. Or, rather, blames her indecision on that belief. Carol's death, accident or suicide, forces everyone into a state of self-reflection that will determine the course the rest of their lives will take.

Character Description
Ken Parker, 32

African American. He has worked for Hutton for three years. For two of those years he has talked openly about leaving and starting his own company. In a world ruled by powerful white men, he feels his blackness very keenly. His cosmetics company would be based on henna African tribal markings, an art form begun by the Egyptians. Ken wants to take control over what he does.

Hutton offers Ken the vice-president position over Carol's husband, Lesley. Ken says he will think about it. Hutton wants Ken to marry Carol should she and Lesley ever get divorced. Ken has, in fact, gone out with Carol and asked her to leave her husband.

He is a control freak, and that causes him to lack romance. He asks Carol to move with him to Turkey, because he thinks they are the kind of people "who could potentially fall in love in a place like that." He sees that they are both people who are sad and dream of something better.

Given Circumstances

Who are they? Ken is addressing the audience, directly.

Where are they? An unnamed city. He could be anywhere in it.

When does this take place? Present day.

Why are they there? Ken is in love with Carol.

What is the pre-beat? Ken is having dinner with Hutton, who offers him the promotion, when Lesley calls to say that Carol has fallen off the roof.

Questions

1. What does Ken want from life?
2. Why has he worked for Hutton for so long if he's unhappy in this company?
3. How much money does Ken make a year?
4. How much power/control does he have in his job?
5. What does control mean to him?
6. Why is he waiting to start his own company?
7. What is it about cosmetics that interests Ken?
8. Hutton accuses him of hating white people. Does he?
9. Hutton treats Ken like the "favorite son." How does this make Ken feel?
10. Is Ken sad?
11. How long has he been attracted to Carol?
12. Is he in love with her?
13. What does she look like?

14. What is Ken's relationship with Lesley like?
15. How does the news of Carol's death affect him?

Carol Mulroney
Stephen Belber

LESLEY

The job is who I am, Carol. It's what I do, it fulfills me and I need you to respect that.

But it's fiscal, right?—it's a fiscal thing, and what *I'm* talking about is spiritual, is you and I understanding each other in a whole new way, so that me working for your father becomes irrelevant. Because listen to me, it doesn't matter what you do, what matters is that the spirit inside you is alive, and that you go to bed each night knowing that nothing is insurmountable, that no problem is answerless as long as you set a goal for tomorrow that no one can talk you out of. You can live in Zimbabwe or on this roof—it doesn't matter. You just have to know that inside you there are solutions. And I'll help you find 'em, but you have to be with me. You have to want it just as bad. I'm serious. I've never been more serious in my life! But, you have to trust me.

And will you not give up on it? Carol?

Thank you. And in the meantime, stop drinking like a fucking fish.

Analysis: *Carol Mulroney*

Type: Dramatic
Synopsis

Carol Mulroney stands on her rooftop looking out over the city, a city she finds "uncompromisingly beautiful." Unfortunately, that beauty is visible only from afar. Up close and inside, it's messy, chaotic, and hurtful. Carol comes to the roof in search of solace and reflection.

She has recently found out that her mother's death was, in fact, a suicide. Already suffering from depression, Carol is pushed even deeper down into it by this discovery. Carol's father, Hutton, runs a major cosmetics corporation. He is powerful and wealthy. Carol's husband, Lesley, works for the company and is up for a promotion. Lesley's co-worker Ken is up for the same job. Hutton has come to Carol to tell her that he is leaning toward promoting Ken over Lesley. Hutton wants to rebuild his relationship with Carol, but she blames him for her mother's suicide.

Carol and Lesley are unhappy. Lesley has always been macho, prone to violence, but he's trying to control that and put his life together. He wants children, but Carol does not. Lesley has been having an affair with their friend Joan.

Ken is in love with Carol. Ken does not want the promotion; he wants to form his own cosmetics company, but he's been saying that for years. Carol drinks a lot, sometimes with her friend Joan, sometimes alone. Occasionally, she paints. Everyone feels stuck.

Carol falls off the roof and dies.

The big question of the play, as posed by Belber, seems to be: who controls our lives? Do we control our own destiny? Are we governed by fate? Do other people's actions affect the course of our lives? Carol blames Hutton for ruining her life, and so she makes every decision based on that belief. Or, rather, blames her indecision on that belief. Carol's death, accident or suicide, forces everyone into a state of self-reflection that will determine the course the rest of their lives will take.

Character Description

Lesley Dane, late 30s

Carol's husband and Hutton's employee. At one time prone to violence, Lesley has recently adopted a New Age, Buddhist-like philosophy on life. He has recently stopped drinking, sober two weeks when the play starts. Despite all the problems with Carol, he professes to love her—even though he's been carrying on a rooftop affair with Joan for an extended period of time, one night a month for three hours. He views this relationship as a temporary escape from his marriage.

Lesley wants to create a rooftop garden in which to grow potatoes. He also wants to raise bees for honey. He feels this will bring a sense of "authenticity" to his life. He wants to renounce everything, "meat, TV, the gym." He is also trying not to curse. He wants kids, Carol does not.

Carol finds him "weird and different." That's what attracted her to him in the first place and why she married him.

Given Circumstances

Who are they? Lesley and Carol are married and having problems.

Where are they? On the rooftop in an unnamed city.

When does this take place? The present.

Why are they there? Carol comes there almost every afternoon to drink.

What is the pre-beat? Carol wants him to quit his job. She wants to separate them completely from her father.

Questions

1. How long have Lesley and Carol been together?
2. What did/does Lesley find attractive about her?
3. How does she feel/look now as compared to then?
4. Why does he want children? How many?
5. How long has Lesley been working for Hutton?
6. What does he like about his job?
7. Does he want the promotion to VP?
8. What is his relationship to Hutton?
9. Does he know Hutton doesn't like him?
10. When did he realize he had anger issues? Was there a specific incident?
11. What does he do to control his temper when it swells?
12. Why does growing potatoes and raising honeybees equal authenticity?
13. How long has he been having an affair with Joan?
14. How is she different from Carol?
15. What does this rooftop mean to him?

Swimming in the Shallows
Adam Bock

NICK

Well that went well. I think it went well. What do you think
I think he liked me.

I'm taking it slow.

After Jason my therapist said maybe I sleep with people
too fast sometimes.

Uh huh. My therapist said that maybe maybe I sleep with
people before I am totally emotionally prepared. Physically
I'm ready fast and so I sleep with them fast but then I wake
up and I'm freaked cause who the hell is this guy? see I'm
slower emotionally. And so then I push them away and then
get scared cause I'm all alone again.

Unless I just want to have sex which is ok my therapist
says. But. If I want to develop something then I have to
develop it. Which is slow. Weird huh.

Think he maybe might be right?

Do you think he liked me?

Analysis: *Swimming in the Shallows*

Type: Comic
Synopsis

Adam Bock sets up the question of this funny, intelligent, and absurd play in the very first scene: What do we really need in life in order to survive and be happy?

Barb, a nurse, has just discovered that Buddhist monks own only eight items. She wants to declutter her life, accordingly, in order to focus on what really matters. A woman of extremes, Barb is by no means having her first phase/craze. Her friends and family do not take her seriously.

The play tracks a group of friends as they try to figure out what exactly they can live with and without. Barb sells, donates, and throws away her possessions, risking the future of her marriage with Bob. Donna tries everything she can to quit smoking so that her longtime girlfriend Carla Carla will marry her. Carla Carla keeps finding ways to put off the wedding. Nick is constantly falling in love too quickly with the wrong guy. This time, he falls in love with a shark (literally, a shark in an aquarium). Nick and Donna have an intense relationship in which they simultaneously feed and challenge each other's bad habits and addictions.

Bock is exploring what it means to love someone and the compromises we make when we choose to spend our lives together. He takes this exploration to absurdly epic proportions in the Nick/Shark relationship. The Shark is, in many ways, an extreme example of all the unavailable, hurtful men Nick has been involved with over the years. Bock illustrates the patterns these people live with and how once they finally recognize them, they can break them and change.

Donna and Carla Carla finally marry. Barb and Bob reconcile when she realizes that she doesn't need to live at such an extreme. The Shark proves he might not be so hurtful after all by living up to promises Nick's other men never did.

Character Description
Nick, 30s

Nick is a typical former "Fatboy" who now defines himself through his relationships with men. He "walks outside and finds a new boyfriend." At the beginning of the play there is Rick, followed by Jack, followed by Jim, followed by Lance, whose name he forgets the next day when he meets Jason. The pattern of these relationships is: we had fun, we had sex, he didn't call. And although he claims to want a relationship more than anything, he sees marriage as "kind of a commitment."

He buys cigarettes for Donna, behind Carla Carla's back, even when she is trying to quit smoking. He is in therapy and quotes his therapist constantly but doesn't really commit to the practice.

He instantly falls in love with The Shark, a mako, and forces Donna (who leads aquarium tours) to introduce him. He wants to be introduced as Nicholas because it sounds more sophisticated. He fears the relationship will fail, but The Shark does, in fact, call him back, and Nick decides to take it slowly this time.

Given Circumstances
Who are they? Nick and Donna are best friends.

Where are they? The aquarium in Twig, Rhode Island.
When does this take place? The present.
Why are they there? Nick is forcing a casual introduction to The Shark through Donna.
What is the pre-beat? Donna has just introduced Nick and The Shark, but the Shark has seemingly taken no notice.

Questions

1. What does Nick look for in a guy?
2. What does Nick find most attractive in a guy?
3. How many guys has Nick been in love with?
4. What does kind of satisfaction does Nick get out of these relationships? Purely physical?
5. Is Nick attracted to his therapist?
6. Although he constantly quotes his therapist, what does Nick think for himself?
7. Why has he never had a relationship last longer than three weeks?
8. What does "commitment" really mean to Nick?
9. How does being a former fat boy affect his perception of himself?
10. How does Nick see himself now?
11. What does he find attractive about The Shark?
12. Why is Donna Nick's best friend?
13. What does he like best about her?
14. What about her drives him crazy?
15. How long have they been friends?

Swimming in the Shallows
Adam Bock

NICK

I once sold paintings door to door.

Horrible. Unbearable.

The paintings. They were landscapes. And one completely ugly clown painting I still

You know Sad clown sad eyes big white mouth head tilted ugh

Me and my friend Shao Mei we were totally broke so we answered an ad Do you want a Career in Art? And since she's a macramé artist and I'm well I'm artistic too

I don't do art but I love art Van Gogh Picasso Michelangelo that guy that paints the sunflowers you know what's his name

Oh yeah Van Gogh so we thought We're perfect. So we go to the place this was outside of Boston and the guy running it piles me and Shao Mei and ten other people in a van and drives us for miles and then when we get there he gives us each a portfolio of ten different paintings Oh they were so ugly The clown Moon over palm trees Moon over waterfall Moon over fir trees Moon over a circus So they're all signed Blunt so I have to pretend I'm Nicholas Blunt cause you know Nick Blunt? that sounds stupid so me and Shao Mei Blunt and ten other Blunts walk around this neighborhood pretending we're poor art school students listen to me I'm just talking and talking

I'm nervous I'm nervous

I had to stop because the clown painting was so ugly it gave me a headache. Plus I walked into a house and they already had one of my paintings. Moon over the mountains right over the sofa.

Horrible.

Analysis: *Swimming in the Shallows*

Type: Seriocomic
Synopsis

Adam Bock sets up the question of this funny, intelligent, and absurd play in the very first scene: What do we really need in life in order to survive and be happy?

Barb, a nurse, has just discovered that Buddhist monks own only eight items. She wants to declutter her life, accordingly, in order to focus on what really matters. A woman of extremes, Barb is by no means having her first phase/craze. Her friends and family do not take her seriously.

The play tracks a group of friends as they try to figure out what exactly they can live with and without. Barb sells, donates, and throws away her possessions, risking the future of her marriage with Bob. Donna tries everything she can to quit smoking so that her longtime girlfriend Carla Carla will marry her. Carla Carla keeps finding ways to put off the wedding. Nick is constantly falling in love too quickly with the wrong guy. This time, he falls in love with a shark (literally, a shark in an aquarium). Nick and Donna have an intense relationship in which they simultaneously feed and challenge each other's bad habits and addictions.

Bock is exploring what it means to love someone and the compromises we make when we choose to spend our lives together. He takes this exploration to absurdly epic proportions in the Nick/Shark relationship. The Shark is, in many ways, an extreme example of all the unavailable, hurtful men Nick has been involved with over the years. Bock illustrates the patterns these people live with and how once they finally recognize them, they can break them and change.

Donna and Carla Carla finally marry. Barb and Bob reconcile when she realizes that she doesn't need to live at such an extreme. The Shark proves he might not be so hurtful after all by living up to promises Nick's other men never did.

Character Description
Nick, 30s

Nick is a typical former "Fatboy" who now defines himself through his relationships with men. He "walks outside and finds a new boyfriend." At the beginning of the play there is Rick, followed by Jack, followed by Jim, followed by Lance, whose name he forgets the next day when he meets Jason. The pattern of these relationships is: we had fun, we had sex, he didn't call. And although Nick claims to want a relationship more than anything, he sees marriage as "kind of a commitment."

He buys cigarettes for Donna, behind Carla Carla's back, even when she is trying to quit smoking. He is in therapy and quotes his therapist constantly but doesn't really commit to the practice.

He instantly falls in love with the The Shark, a mako, and forces Donna (who leads aquarium tours) to introduce him. He wants to be introduced as Nicholas because it sounds more sophisticated. He fears the relationship will fail, but The Shark does, in fact, call him back, and Nick decides to take it slowly this time.

Given Circumstances

Who are they? Nick and The Shark are on their first date.

Where are they? The beach in Twig, Rhode Island.

When does this take place? The present.

Why are they there? The Shark has just talked about how he loves to swim.

What is the pre-beat? The Shark just told Nick he sold Avon's Skin So Soft door-to-door.

Questions

1. What does The Shark look like?
2. What does Nick find attractive about The Shark?
3. Where does Nick want this relationship to go?
4. What does this beach look like?
5. Is it a warm or cold day on the beach? What does the air feel like?
6. Does Nick like to swim? Is he a good swimmer?
7. What does Nick want to do with his life?

8. Does he view himself as successful?

9. How does he want The Shark to see him?

10. Why does he tell this story?

11. What is he revealing about himself through telling this?

12. What does Shao Mei look like? Are she and Nick still friends?

13. What did the paintings look like? Visualize them.

14. Nick used to work at a fast-food joint on this beach. Why take The Shark here and point it out?

15. Is Nick in love with The Shark already?

The Pride
Alexi Kaye Campbell

PHILIP

Are you finished? Is there anything else you wish to discuss?
Or am I free to go now?

You asked me not to leave. You obviously felt a burning need to communicate these disparate and disturbing
thoughts to me, and I'm simply asking you if you've now
finished.

If you're asking me if I think Oliver Henshaw is a homosexual, I really wouldn't know. I haven't given it a moment's
thought. His private life, after all, is none of my business,
and neither do I think it should be any of yours. I will try and
explain to myself your somewhat strange behavior tonight by
the fact that you have clearly been upset by this man Coveley's death. This, combined with the possibility that you had
a few too many glasses of wine can go some way to justifying
what can only be described as an outburst of irrationality.
Now if you'll excuse me, I really do need to return to bed.

Good night.

Analysis: *The Pride*

Type: Dramatic
Synopsis

"Do you believe in change?" Oliver asks his ex-boyfriend, Philip, toward the end of Alexi Kaye Campbell's time-shifting drama. The year is 2008, and the two men, along with their best friend, Sylvia, are at London's Pride celebration. Alternating between 2008 and 1958, Campbell clearly depicts how much life has changed for gay men in fifty years. No longer condemned to live in the shadows or resort to conversion therapy, they may now live out in the open and with pride.

In 1958 Campbell introduces us to married couple Philip and Sylvia. Once an actress, Sylvia is now a children's-book illustrator. She invites Oliver, the book's author, to join her and Philip for dinner. At the first meeting, Oliver shares a story about an experience he had while traveling in Greece. He went out one morning to visit the famous Oracle at Delphi. While there, he heard a voice whisper that everything would be all right. Oliver interpreted that to mean in fifty or five hundred years there will be a "deeper understanding of certain aspects of our nature." He is, of course, alluding to the fact that homosexuality won't be discriminated against. Oliver and Philip feel an electric charge between them.

That scene ends and we are transported to 2008 and a man named Oliver is having a sexual encounter with a man dressed as a Nazi. It turns out that this Oliver has recently been broken up with by his boyfriend, Philip. Modern Oliver cannot stop himself from having sex with strangers. He picks them up online, in the park, in the bathroom. Philip finds out about it and, after a year and a half, ends their relationship for the third and final time. Philip, thinking Oliver is out of town on business, walks in on Oliver and the faux Nazi.

As the play continues to jump back and forth in time, we see the dissolution of Philip and Sylvia's marriage, sparked by a secret affair between Philip and Oliver. Philip breaks off his relationship with Oliver and then violently rapes him. Philip goes to a doctor to seek conversion therapy. Sylvia leaves Philip.

In present-day London, we see Oliver attempt to figure out why he behaves the way he does as his best friend, Sylvia, tries to forge a life of her own and Philip tries to recover from Oliver's betrayal.

Character Description
Philip, mid-30s
Sylvia's husband. He sells property for a living. His line of work frustrates him. He inherited the business from his father. His older brother was being groomed to take over but was killed in a car accident. Philip had been useless and aimless until then.

He is envious of Sylvia and Oliver, their ability to "do something creative . . . being able to invest a certain amount of passion in what you do for a living."

Philip always dreamed of immigrating somewhere, somewhere far away like Australia or Canada. The apartment is filled with books on Kenya and Rhodesia, but in reality he's never been farther away than Brighton.

He suffers often from bad dreams. He was passive and melancholy at the first dinner with Oliver.

Given Circumstances

Who are they? Philip and Sylvia, a married couple.

Where are they? Their London apartment.

When does this take place? 1958.

Why are they there? Philip met Oliver for the first time and they all dined together.

What is the pre-beat? Sylvia brings up a friend of hers, Richard Coveley, whom she read killed himself recently. She remembers Philip took exception to him, much like he seems to take exception to Oliver.

Questions

1. How long have Philip and Sylvia been together?
2. How did they meet?
3. What is their home life like?
4. Do they have a romantic/sexual relationship?
5. Does Philip love Sylvia?
6. What does he need from her?
7. How long has Philip had feelings, sexual or otherwise, for men?
8. Has he ever acted on them?
9. What did Richard Coveley look like?
10. Was Philip attracted to him?

11. Did he act on it?
12. What does Oliver look like?
13. What does Philip find attractive about him?
14. What was Philip thinking about at dinner when he got quiet and melancholy?
15. Do Philip and Sylvia fight often?

99 Histories
Julia Cho

JOE

You know what your problem is? You're like Russia.

It's like when Napoleon went to war with Russia. He amasses this huge army and drives into Russian territory, hungry to fight. He can't wait. So he gets his men ready and then the next morning, he goes out to the battlefield and charges the enemy. Except the field is totally empty. There isn't a Russian to be seen. He keeps chasing them farther and farther into the interior, and they just keep withdrawing until finally Napoleon and his men are starving and exhausted and defeated.

I am not your enemy. I'm just saying that you have a habit of doing that. Withdrawing. You know I tried. Even when we were together, I always felt alone. And I'd only brought so many supplies with me and they only lasted so long.

Analysis: *99 Histories*

Type: Seriocomic
Synopsis
Eunice is a self-described "bum." Currently New York City–based but she travels constantly. She drops her mother, Sah-Jin,

postcards from time to time but never calls or visits—until she finds herself unexpectedly pregnant.

Eunice stops by her ex-boyfriend Joe's apartment to return her keys, and she tells him that she's four weeks pregnant with his child. He offers to help out in any way she needs, but Eunice has already worked out everything through the adoption agency. Then she tells him she is going to Los Angeles for a bit to be with her mother. Eunice leaves without giving Joe her number out there but promising she'll call.

Once Eunice gets to L.A., she finds herself confronting her own tendency to withdraw, coupled with her mother's tendency to withhold information about her past. As Eunice begins writing long letters to her unborn child (including a list of great books and plays to read), she finds a box of mementos. She believes the woman in a photo to be her mother and a young American officer to be a man Sah-Jin once loved in her village.

Sah-Jin unfolds a story in which the young officer, Daniel, came to the village and asked for music lessons in exchange for English lessons. These stories, along with flashbacks of Eunice as a young child, are told in vivid flashbacks.

Meanwhile, Sah-Jin invites a young doctor from her church, Paul, to dinner in an attempt to set the two young people up. Sah-Jin knows Paul is married, but this doesn't stop her. She has grown close to Paul at church, even bringing him home-cooked meals. Paul reveals that he used to watch Eunice play cello when she was young and was enthralled by her talent. They become friends but not lovers.

Eunice pushes her mother to reveal more and more about the past, including the "illness" that made her stop playing cello once and for all. Eunice wants the secrets of the past unlocked so she can decide what to do with the baby. Ultimately, the two women begin to find common ground, although we are left uncertain about where Eunice will go or what she will do.

Character Description
Joe, late 20s
A New York guy, originally from Vermont, who is open and communicative. The kind of guy who stays friends with his exes. "Breaking up doesn't change who you are," he says. "You still like who that person is, right?"

When they were dating, Joe brought Eunice a curtain rod to hang a proper window treatment rather than the blanket on a string she was using. He knew it was her from half a word on the phone. He asked Eunice to move in with him. She didn't. They broke up.

He is shocked by Eunice's pregnancy, since they always took precautions when having sex. He immediately offers support, emotional or financial. He is taken aback that Eunice is dropping this news and then leaving for L.A. but asks her to call him and keep him updated once she's there.

Given Circumstances
Who are they? Joe and Eunice are ex-lovers who have recently broken up.
Where are they? Joe's apartment.

When does this take place? The present.

Why are they there? Eunice is returning her keys to his place.

What is the pre-beat? Eunice tells Joe she is going to L.A. but doesn't tell him why.

Questions

1. How long has Joe lived in NYC?
2. How is NYC different from Vermont?
3. What does he do for a living?
4. Where in NYC does he live?
5. What does his apartment look like?
6. How many women has he dated in that time?
7. How many of those women has he been in love with?
8. How did he meet Eunice?
9. How long did they date?
10. Has he ever lived with a girlfriend before?
11. Did/does Joe love her?
12. What does Eunice look like?
13. What did/does Joe find attractive about her?
14. Is she the first Korean American woman he's dated?
15. Why did he stay with her if he found her uncommunicative?

The Language Archive
Julia Cho

GEORGE

I am a linguist. This is my trade. Lots of people ask me if this means I can speak a lot of languages. And I do have a passable acquaintance with Greek, Latin, French, Cantonese, Spanish, Dutch, Portuguese and Esperanto. Of these all, I am perhaps most fond of Esperanto, that made-up, utopian dream of a language. Proudly, I say, *"La vivo sen Esperanto estas neimagebla al mi!"* Life without Esperanto is unimaginable to me! So.

What is death to a linguist? What is, so to speak, worth mourning? I know this: There are sixty-nine hundred languages in the world. More than half are expected to die within the next century. In fact, it's estimated that every two weeks, a language dies. I don't know about you, but this statistic moves me far more than any statistic on how many animals die or how many people die in a given time, in a given place. Because when we say a language dies, we are talking about a whole world, a whole way of life. It is the death of imagination, of memory.

It makes me much sadder than I could ever possibly express. Even with all my languages, there still aren't the right words.

Analysis: *The Language Archive*

Type: Dramatic
Synopsis

George and Mary are married. George is worried about Mary. Although she used to be an upbeat person, she has recently become very sad. She seems to cry all the time, whether she's washing the dishes or sleeping. Conversely, Mary thinks George is the one who is sad, but when she tries to explain why, he won't let her get a word in edgewise.

George has been finding little notes all over the house. Notes that say things like: "Husband or throw pillow? Wife or hot water bottle? Marriage or an old cardigan?" But Mary denies that she's the one leaving them.

The irony of the situation is that George is a linguist. He studies languages, speaks dozens of languages, collects dead languages, but he cannot find the words to communicate with his wife. And so, Mary leaves him.

The language archive where George works is a collection of some five hundred-plus tapes and recordings and remnants of languages that no longer exist. His assistant, Emma, is deeply in love with him. She is studying Esperanto but can't learn it. Perhaps, her teacher posits, she has some psychological block, since "all second languages are learned out of love."

George has invited an older couple, Alta and Restin, to the archive, as they are among the last speakers of a dying language called Elloway. Unfortunately for George, they are in a huge fight and, when they fight, speak only English to each other.

They use terrible, hurtful words when they fight because English is an ugly language and only angry people speak it. Their language is "too sacred" for angry talk. They are fighting because Restin hasn't been eating Alta's food and she is insulted. It turns out that he is sick, and once he is hospitalized and treated, they make up. The couple explain to George that "language dies before words."

Mary makes one last attempt with George. She stops by the archive, but he simply cannot find the words to say "I love you." She leaves for good. At the train platform she meets an old man who gives her a bread starter. This man has been a very unhappy baker for many years and is leaving his business. Mary takes the starter and becomes a successful and happy baker.

George and Emma work together for many years but never become lovers. Alta and Restin remain together to the end of their lives, bickering with love to the very end. George finds Mary and leaves her a tape with a symphony of "I love yous" spoken in different languages, but she doesn't return to him. He, after many years, finds one final note from her, but it is blank.

Character Description
George, 30s
A linguist. He thinks his wife is sad because she's been crying all the time, but she thinks he is the sad one. He can't say, or doesn't understand that Mary needs him to say, "I love you." When Mary tells him she is leaving, his entire body shakes but all he can say

is, " . . . Don't . . . Go . . . ?" He doesn't know how to interpret the notes Mary leaves for him.

George lies on the floor of his lab, in a waking dream, with scraps of words and language everywhere — things he should have said to Mary.

Given Circumstances

Who are they? George is talking directly to the audience.

Where are they? George and Mary's house.

When does this take place? The present.

Why are they there? It is their home.

What is the pre-beat? Mary has just told George she's leaving.

Questions

1. How long have George and Mary been a couple?
2. How did they meet?
3. What does George love about her?
4. What does Mary look like?
5. What does he think is the cause of her sadness?
6. When did he notice a change in Mary?
7. If Mary is crying all the time, why doesn't George comfort her?
8. Has he ever said "I love you" to her?
9. Why doesn't George suggest therapy?
10. Is George happy?
11. Has he ever thought Mary would leave him?

12. Does Mary mean anything to him besides the usual practicalities of married life?
13. What do these notes mean to him?
14. Why can't/doesn't George cry?
15. What is their home like?

The Language Archive
Julia Cho

GEORGE

Mary. Do you know how language dies?

One. Natural disaster. A typhoon, say, knocking out an entire village that is the only place where a certain language is spoken. Two. Social assimilation. When speakers of two languages choose the more socially dominant one to the point where their children speak only that language and lose the other one completely.

I speak many languages. But I do not speak the one my grandmother spoke. Why? Because my parents didn't really speak it. And didn't care if I really spoke it. Because it was not the socially dominant language. Thus: I never cared to learn it. It was the one language I never cared to learn. And now it's too late. So, Mary. There is a certain language . . . our language . . . and. If you don't come back, I can't speak it anymore. Do you understand? We are the only two speakers of that language. And if you don't come back, the language will die and no one on earth will ever speak it again.

For instance, the phrase: "Will somebody please take out the garbage?" Depending on tone it can mean: "You jerk, take out the garbage!" Or, "I feel lonely." Or, "It's our anniversary next week, I hope you remember." Or, "A world without you is unimaginable to me." Mary. Mary. Will somebody please take out the garbage?

Analysis: *The Language Archive*

Type: Dramatic
Synopsis

George and Mary are married. George is worried about Mary. Although she used to be an upbeat person, she has recently become very sad. She seems to cry all the time, whether she's washing the dishes or sleeping. Conversely, Mary thinks George is the one who is sad, but when she tries to explain why, he won't let her get a word in edgewise.

George has been finding little notes all over the house. Notes that say things like: "Husband or throw pillow? Wife or hot water bottle? Marriage or an old cardigan?" But Mary denies that she's the one leaving them.

The irony of the situation is that George is a linguist. He studies languages, speaks dozens of languages, collects dead languages, but he cannot find the words to communicate with his wife. And so, Mary leaves him.

The language archive where George works is a collection of some five hundred-plus tapes and recordings and remnants of languages that no longer exist. His assistant, Emma, is deeply in love with him. She is studying Esperanto but can't learn it. Perhaps, her teacher posits, she has some psychological block, since "all second languages are learned out of love."

George has invited an older couple, Alta and Restin, to the archive, as they are among the last speakers of a dying language called Elloway. Unfortunately for George, they are in a huge fight and, when they fight, speak only English to each other. They use terrible, hurtful words when they fight because English is an ugly language and only angry people speak it. Their language is "too sacred" for angry talk. They are fighting because Restin hasn't been eating Alta's food and she is insulted. It turns out that he is sick, and once he is hospitalized and treated, they make up. The couple explain to George that "language dies before words."

Mary makes one last attempt with George. She stops by the archive, but he simply cannot find the words to say "I love you." She leaves for good. At the train platform she meets an old man who gives her a bread starter. This man has been a very unhappy baker for many years and is leaving his business. Mary takes the starter and becomes a successful and happy baker.

George and Emma work together for many years but never become lovers. Alta and Restin remain together to the end of their lives, bickering with love to the very end. George finds Mary and leaves her a tape with a symphony of "I love yous" spoken in different languages, but she doesn't return to him. He, after many years, finds one final note from her, but it is blank.

Character Description
George, 30s.
A linguist. He thinks his wife is sad because she's been crying all the time, but she thinks he is the sad one. He can't say, or doesn't understand that Mary needs him to say, "I love you." When Mary

tells him she is leaving, his entire body shakes but all he can say is, " . . . Don't . . . Go . . . ?" He doesn't know how to interpret the notes Mary leaves for him.

George lies on the floor of his lab, in a waking dream, with scraps of words and language everywhere — things he should have said to Mary.

Given Circumstances

Who are they? George and Mary are married but separated.

Where are they? Mary's business, the Blue Tulip Bakery.

When does this take place? The present.

Why are they there? George searched everywhere for Mary when he left. His assistant, Emma, stumbled upon her here.

What is the pre-beat? George starts to tear up a bit, but Mary doesn't see because she's kneading bread.

Questions

1. How long were George and Mary a couple?
2. How long has it been since Mary left?
3. What does Mary look like?
5. Does she look different than when he last saw her?
6. Does George miss her?
7. What does he miss most about her?
8. Does he still sleep on his side of the bed?
9. Does he expect her to get back together with him?
10. He put together a tape of "I love yous" in different languages but doesn't say the words himself. Why?
11. Does he love her?

12. Is his work more important to him than he marriage?
13. What has life been like for George since Mary left?
14. What did he do with the notes Mary left him?
15. What will happen if he doesn't win her back?

Living Room in Africa
Bathsheba Doran

ANTHONY

I have seen a doctor. I am well. A good doctor. In the city. I do not have the disease. I checked. I was scared after that night, Edward. I went to this doctor. The doctor says I am lucky. He tells me many people will die. It is like you said. You get it from the blood.

My wife, she will die. And the child. He is sure. My wife, she says I must come to you. My wife says it's OK for me to leave. She will stay here alone. It is best. She says. She says it, Edward.

You, you live in this big house. You don't understand how it is for me. How it is for everyone. Where I live . . . you do not know, Edward, what I come from every day when I come to the gallery. Everyone where I live is dying! There is silence everywhere while people wait for their death to come for them. No one speaks about it, we just walk through it, we are stepping over bodies to walk to the road. No one is clearing the bodies, Edward. There are people lying outside their house, you don't know if they sleep or if they are dead now.

There is a smell and there is nowhere in the village you can go that does not have that smell. Some people think you can catch it just from the smell. I think that too, sometimes, at night. But I do not understand why I think that because the smell is sweet.

Step off the road and walk down the hill and you would see Africa. There are hundreds of families. With no running water, no proper doors, or windows, or beds, Edward, or chairs like these! It is nothing! Nothing! You would refuse to live this way.

I refuse it too, Edward.

Analysis: *Living Room in Africa*

Type: Dramatic
Synopsis

Edward and his partner, Marie, live in a large, dilapidated house about an hour's drive from an unnamed African city and a twenty-minute walk to the nearest village. Natives of England, Edward and Marie have lived all over the world. Edward has come here now to open an art gallery in a village where there is no running water. Marie is a poet. Although they live as a couple, theirs is not a romantic relationship. There are many veiled references to Edward's homosexuality. However, Edward and Marie love (or have loved) one another and depend on each other for support.

At the beginning of the play, the couple have been here a few months but they are blind to the atrocities that surround them. AIDS is killing people in the village, but Marie knows only that there is a "disease" present. There is a strange screaming outside the house that no one can define. The water is polluted. There is no educational system. There are no jobs. Edward's one solution is to build a pool for the villagers, since they can't swim in the river because of parasites. When a child cracks his head open in the pool, bleeding profusely, the pool needs to be cleared and drained immediately. No one refills it.

Edward and Marie can't see, or refuse to see, the reality of the world around them.

Anthony, a local who works for Edward, is desperately trying to get Edward to take him away with them when they leave Africa. He is good, honest, and a hardworking professional. It is, through Anthony and Nsugo, the cook, that the realities of life in Africa are most vividly illustrated.

Marie is working on a sprawling poem but won't let anyone read it. She chews a native hallucinogenic stick to escape her depression and the reality of her unfulfilled relationship with Edward. She finds solace and hope in her friendship with Nsugo, who has two children living with AIDS and two who have died from the disease.

When Edward's eyes are finally opened to the reality and hopelessness of the situation, he decides to pack up and leave as soon as possible without opening the art gallery. Marie, feeling she has nowhere to go, and no reason to go with him, wants to stay and help. It is Anthony's suicide, on their grounds, that forces Marie to confront the awful reality of the world and to flee with Edward.

Character Description
Anthony, mid-20s–mid 30s
A native African and a contractor by trade. He has helped build a supermarket, the swimming pool, and, now, the art gallery in his

village. He wants to get out and start a new life for himself in another, better country. He sees Edward as the vehicle to achieving
this. He is hardworking and productive. He can procure women
in the town as prostitutes should anyone be interested. He has
been married for one year and has a daughter. He does not know
how AIDS is transmitted and does not use condoms because he
is Christian. He views AIDS as a punishment for wrongdoing.

Given Circumstances

Who are they? Anthony is a contractor, and Edward is his boss.
Where are they? The living room of Anthony's house in Africa.
When does this take place? The present.
Why are they there? Anthony has rushed over in the rain from
the doctor's office.
What is the pre-beat? Anthony has asked Marie to leave the room
so she can speak to Edward in private.

Questions

   1. What has life in Africa been like for Anthony?
   2. When did he realize how bad things were?
   3. How many friends/family members has he watched die?
   4. Where did he learn his trade?
   5. Where did he learn English?
   6. What is the extent of his education?
   7. What does Christianity/God mean to him?
   8. How does his religion influence his life?
   9. Where did he meet his wife?
  10. What does she look like? What is her name?

11. Does he love her?

12. Does he have sex with other women? Men

13. What does his daughter look like? What is her name?

14. Why does Edward represent his means of escape?

15. When does suicide become an option for Anthony?

Asuncion
Jesse Eisenberg

STUART

You don't do anything, Edgar. Would you shut the fuck up about Cambodia! You went there by accident. For two fucking nights when your little freshman spring break plane to Bangkok got rerouted.

You don't have convictions, Edgar. You have opinions. They're two very different things. Sit down!

I took Asuncion up here because she wanted to meet her new brother. Yes, we were in a bit of trouble, which is my issue — not yours! — but when I told her I thought she should stay in a hotel for a few days, she starts crying, thinking that my white family won't accept my new Filipina bride. And I understood why. Because, frankly, white people have kind of been pricks over the years. But whatever you did to her this week, however you made her feel, makes you the worst kind of white prick there is. Because you call yourself a pussy, when you're actually a prick.

Analysis: *Asuncion*

Type: Seriocomic
Synopsis

Vinny and Edgar live in a Binghamton, New York, attic apartment. They are not romantically involved. Vinny is a professor at the university. Edgar was, at one time, Vinny's teaching assistant. He started living in the living room of Vinny's apartment soon after graduation. Vinny is a major stoner.

Edgar is young, naive, and innocent. He calls himself a humanitarian and a journalist, but he has no real goals. His brother, Stuart, shows up on his doorstep unexpectedly one day. Stuart has just married and wants his wife, Asuncion, to stay with Edgar and Vinny while he clears up some business involving Asuncion's family.

Asuncion is a beautiful Filipina woman. Edgar puts up a fight about the situation, saying the apartment is not his. But Vinny has no problem with the arrangement and says Asuncion can stay as long as necessary. Vinny and Stuart used to party together and pick up girls when Stuart would come to visit Edgar in college. Edgar wants to know what the "business" is that Stuart needs to clear up, but Stuart won't say. Edgar is convinced that Stuart acquired Asuncion as a sex slave and that's why he's being so shady about the situation.

Vinny convinces Edgar that he should write a story about Asuncion, detailing her life story and how she got to America. Edgar thinks this is a great idea and says he will do so, but without her knowledge. He begins a very conspicuous crusade to get information from her, but he always ends up talking more about himself than actually getting information from her. Meanwhile, much to Edgar's chagrin, Vinny and Asuncion really hit it off, becoming fast friends and, Edgar suspects, lovers.

One night the three roommates drop acid. Edgar compulsively cleans the bathroom while Asuncion and Vinny trip in the living room. Soon, though, Vinny reveals Edgar's secret plot. The two men get into a fistfight that ends with Asuncion pouring hot water on the two of them.

Stuart returns to get Asuncion. He gives Edgar a check and Asuncion gives him the cash she has left, $250. Stuart reveals that Asuncion's family business involved the selling of cheap antibiotics from the Philippines. He was clearing her from any involvement. Edgar is lost to find his conspiracy theories shattered. Vinny tells Edgar to go somewhere with the money. Edgar researches a trip to Tanzania, but as the lights fade he doesn't move.

Character Description
Stuart Hirschhorn, mid- to late 30s

Edgar's older brother and recently married to Asuncion. Although his job isn't specified, it's clear that he has money. He is the opposite of Edgar in every way and says to him, "I want to be happy, Edgar. I don't want to be like you. And that doesn't make me bad. It makes me practical." He offers Edgar money to get out of this apartment and make a better life for himself, but Edgar refuses. He sees Edgar as morally superior even though he does nothing.

Met Asuncion online and it was love at first sight. He loves Sunny, as he calls Asuncion, to "peaches." He watches what she eats, scolding her for coming in with a bag from McDonald's. He lost his virginity to a prostitute in Red Bank on his prom night.

Given Circumstances
Who are they? Stuart is Edgar's older brother and polar opposite.
Where are they? The living room of Vinny's apartment, where Edgar lives in Binghamton, New York.
When does this take place? The present.
Why are they there? Stuart has come to take Asuncion home.
What is the pre-beat? Edgar was convinced Sunny was involved in something illegal, and Stuart reveals what the real situation was. When Edgar finds out, he claims he's going to turn her in.

Questions
1. What is the age difference between Stuart and Edgar?
2. How does that affect their relationship?
3. What does Edgar look like? Does he take care of himself/his appearance?
4. Does Stuart take care of his appearance? How is he different from Edgar?
5. What does this apartment look like?
6. Where does Stuart live?
7. What does it look like in comparison to this place?
8. What does Stuart do for a living?
9. What did Stuart's online profile say?
10. What did Sunny's say?

11. How long have Stuart and Asuncion known each other? The implication is this has happened very quickly, but just how quickly?

12. Is he in love with her?

13. What does she look like?

14. What exactly did Stuart have to do to extradite Sunny from her family business?

15. Why doesn't he have any other place or friends to leave Sunny with?

Bethany
Laura Marks

GARY

What are they teaching her in school? They're socializing her. They're teaching her not to hit other kids, and to keep her skirt down, and raise her hand when she has to go to the bathroom. Every single thing her body wants to do is getting smashed down by the military-industrial complex, and the worst part is that it happens all day, every day, to everyone, and everyone just lets it happen.

Look at you: you go around all day with that big, fake smile pasted on across your face, selling people a bunch of crap they don't need so you can go buy crap you don't need. "I just have to make this sale." You completely bought the government messages. But what happens now? Are you gonna just curl up and die? Or are you gonna fight back? Because when you have to struggle for food and shelter, just like we did millions of years ago, boom! You start getting your mind back. And we have to take advantage of this time and fight the system until we obliterate it. You and me, we'll never recover a hundred percent; but your daughter's young; she might still have a chance . . . You see, it won't be a collective society anymore where technology controls the masses. It'll just be individuals and small groups. And when the centers of technology and finance go down, we need to be ready to survive. Small, nomadic groups have the best shot at it. I know how to trap food and I know all the edible plants.

I'll tell you what you should do. You pick her up from school. You say, "Don't worry, honey, we're never going back there again." Then the three of us get in your car and we start driving. We drive until we hit the wilderness. Someplace without all this EMF radiation. We build a shelter. Or find one. And we've got the seeds of a new society. XX . . . XX . . . XY.

Analysis: *Bethany*

Type: Dramatic
Synopsis
Laura Marks's short, powerful play explores just how far a mother will go to protect her child.

The play takes place in a small, unnamed suburban town in 2009 during the height of the foreclosure crisis and economic decline. The play opens with Crystal using a plastic ID card to break into a seemingly unoccupied house. Unfortunately for her, the home has a resident. Gary, homeless and dirty, has already claimed ownership of the building but offers to let Crystal occupy the downstairs since he mainly stays on the second floor. Torn at first, Crystal has little choice and, luckily, the electricity and water are still on and working here.

Crystal is currently employed as a sales associate for Saturn Automobiles. She works on commission, so every sale matters.

Charlie, a middle-aged motivational speaker, comes in often to look at a particular vehicle valued at $32,594 plus tax. The commission on this would be a major upswing for Crystal. She recently lost her own house, and, after spending two nights in a car with her daughter, she lost her child as well. Bethany, five years old, is now in foster care. Crystal is forbidden any contact with her until the state approves her current living situation.

Crystal attempts to butter up Gary by offering him food and buying some essentials for the house. She needs him to leave when the social worker comes by to see the place. He doesn't deem this situation necessary and decides to stay, masquerading as a plumber. The social worker buys the act but needs Crystal to make some more adjustments to the house, all of which cost more money than she has.

Meanwhile, Charlie asks Crystal out to dinner. He drives her home and says that he'll buy the car if Crystal sleeps with him. Gary, listening to the whole conversation from another room, physically threatens Charlie with a two-by-four, but Crystal stops him and goes off with Charlie to a motel.

The following day Charlie's wife, Patricia, shows up at the dealership and confronts Crystal. Patricia tells Crystal that Charlie has no money and no one will hire him. Patricia has smartly invested her own money. Crystal invents a long-term affair with Charlie and blackmails Patricia out of some $10,000, saying she'll end the affair and leave town.

When Crystal arrives home that evening, after quitting her job, she finds that Gary has trashed the place. The two get into a fight. Crystal pushes him down and beats him to death with his own two-by-four.

Character Description
Gary, 30s
Illegally occupying a foreclosed home because he just needs a place to lay his head. He doesn't go anywhere unless he absolutely needs to. He wears shabby clothes and looks like he hasn't held a job in a long time. When Crystal arrives, he hasn't showered in a while because he forgets to do so. He hasn't eaten in a while and wolfs down a package of nuts Crystal gives him. He meditates. He masturbates when he needs to. He eats C rations that he buys at the army-navy store. He carries a two-by-four for protection.

Given Circumstances
Who are they? Gary and Crystal are living together but not romantically involved.
Where are they? The kitchen of a foreclosed house they occupy illegally.
When does this take place? 2009.
Why are they there? A social worker just came to view the house.
What is the pre-beat? Gary has just discovered Crystal has a child.

Questions
1. How long has Gary been staying in this house?
2. How does he know a house is empty?
3. How does he get in?
4. How much money does he have?

5. Where does he get money?

6. How long has he been living like this?

7. Where is he from?

8. What does Crystal look like?

9. Why does Gary let her stay?

10. Is he attracted to her?

11. Is he attracted to anyone?

12. What does he do all day long?

13. What was his childhood like?

14. Does he ever talk to his family?

15. Why doesn't he just move to the wilderness?

Next Fall
Geoffrey Nauffts

BRANDON

I like black men. That's all I've ever been attracted to. I
don't know why, it just is. And . . .

Luke's not black.

I was never in love with him, Adam. Our friendship
ended because we both chose for it to. There was nothing
"unrequited" about it.

I've been struggling with this stuff my whole life. When
I met Luke, it was like, finally someone who understood.
Finally someone who I felt safe with. But somewhere along
the line things started to shift. When you two were just
hooking up, it was one thing, but when it turned into something, well, more . . . Look, I understand the need to act
on it, believe me, but to choose the lifestyle? To live like it
was . . . right, I guess?

Well, that's where we go our separate ways. And Luke un-
derstands that. It took us a while, but we've made our peace.

Analysis: *Next Fall*

Type: Dramatic
Synopsis

Luke, an aspiring actor, has been hit by a car and critically injured. His friends and family gather in an NYC waiting room for word on his chances of recovery. The cab driver that hit Luke was uninsured and driving illegally. Luke's divorced (but mostly friendly) parents have flown in from Tallahassee, Florida, to be there. Luke's longtime (and fifteen-years-older) lover Adam was out of town at his high school reunion and came back as quickly as possible.

Luke grew up Christian and remains incredibly religious. This has been a strong point of contention between Adam and him for the duration of their five-year relationship. Adam wants Luke to love him more then he loves God. Adam wants Luke to stop praying after they have sex. Adam's last words to Luke before leaving for his reunion were: "I don't think I can do this any more."

Adam also spent a lot of time asking Luke to come out to his parents. Luke never did. Because of this, Luke's parents don't really know who Adam is, and they certainly don't understand his fevered desire to be near Luke at this point in time. As Luke's health worsens, Adam knows that Luke would not want to be kept alive on life support. His parents do not know this.

Geoffrey Naufft's play, filled with humor and pathos, is told partly in the present and partly in flashback. He slowly fills in the details in the complex portrait of a relationship rooted firmly in love but filled with tension. Adam has spent the past five years wanting to be *the* priority in Luke's life and finds himself in the same position as Luke lies close to death. In the end, Luke's parents take him off life support and his organs are given to those in need.

Character Description
Brandon, 30
Brandon is an NYC property developer and formerly Luke's best friend. In fact, it was Luke who convinced Brandon to move here from Washington, D.C. When Brandon worked in D.C., he wore only red, white, and blue ties with his suits.

He is very successful and rich.

He is very religious and carries a Bible with him. Luke's mother has taken that Bible for comfort.

There has always been tension between Adam and Brandon.

Brandon, not Adam, was Luke's emergency contact. Brandon was the first person the hospital called.

He hasn't spoken to Luke in three years.

Brandon, at one time, really liked a married guy he met in an online chat room. He told this to Luke, who then told Adam.

Given Circumstances
Who are they? Adam is Luke's boyfriend; Brandon is Luke's former best friend.

Where are they? A bench in Central Park.

When does this take place? Four years into Adam and Luke's relationship.

Why are they there? Adam called Brandon to meet.

What is the pre-beat? Adam asks Brandon what he can do about the fact that Luke prays after sex.

Questions

1. When did Adam call Brandon?
2. What were Brandon's feelings about this meeting?
3. Does Brandon like Adam?
4. Is Brandon jealous of Adam and Luke's relationship?
5. What does Adam look like?
6. Does Brandon miss his friendship with Luke?
7. What does he miss most about it?
8. What part of Central Park are they in?
9. What's the view from their bench?
10. What exactly is property development?
11. Does Brandon like his job?
12. What does God mean to Brandon?
13. Why does he let his religion determine the parameters of his love life?
14. Is Brandon embarrassed about his attraction to black men?
15. What is Brandon's sex life like?

Crumbs from the Table of Joy
Lynn Nottage

GODFREY

My gals are going to have the best. They're gonna rise above you and I.

When you're on my time clock, eating out of my icebox, sleeping under my roof, Father Divine is your leader. His word is grace. You don't like it you can git the . . . you can leave us at peace.

I left Florida for a reason, couldn't breathe, couldn't think, couldn't do nothing but go to work, make my dime and drink it down on Friday night. Then I found something that gave me inspiration, gave me strength to make a change. May not be like your change, revolution! Oh, but it do feel that big to me. It soothed my pain and that's all I want right now. It took all the strength I had to take these gals on a train, out their wooden doors and place 'em here in brick and concrete. And I think I deserve some respect and you're trying me, you're trying me.

I smell the liquor and the sweat. I see the jukebox swirling and the cats laughing. I can hear the big sister on stage hollering out her song. Go on, sing! But I ain't going there. Taste my lips puffing on a Cuba, talking out me ass.

Feel my hands 'round a woman's hips, swaying to the beat.

But I ain't there!

Analysis: *Crumbs from the Table of Joy*

Type: Dramatic
Synopsis

Brooklyn, 1950. After the death of his wife, Godfrey Crump moves from Pensacola, Florida, with his two teenaged girls. Godfrey travels to Brooklyn in search of Father Divine, a mail-order preacher, whom he wrote to upon Sandra's passing. The preacher responded in turn, "curing" Godfrey of his grief. Father Divine's letter was postmarked "Brooklyn, NY," so Godfrey picked up his family and resettled.

Ernestine, seventeen, and Ermina, fifteen, are not accustomed to living in an integrated world. Their upstairs neighbors are a Jewish couple who pay the girls to shut the lights for them on the Sabbath. Ernestine, destined to be the first high school graduate in her family, escapes her pain and fear by going to the movies. Ermina is the more assertive and combative of the two girls. Just as the family is beginning to find their footing, they are knocked off balance by the appearance of Sandra's sister, Lily. Lily shows up unannounced, with all of her bags, and moves in. She has lived in NYC for many years, in Harlem, and is rumored to be a revolutionary.

Lily has promised her mother she would help take care of the girls. And she does bring a much-needed dose of femininity and a modern sensibility to the apartment. However, her appearance seems to be more motivated by the fact that she is homeless and jobless. The fact that she and Godfrey used to be lovers further complicates the situation. Lily represents all the aspects of Godfrey's old life that he is trying to escape: alcohol, womanizing, juke joints, late nights, et cetera.

Cracking under this stress, Godfrey disappears for a few days. When he returns, he enters with a Caucasian, German-born woman named Gerte whom he explains he met on the subway and proceeded to marry.

Gerte tries hard to build a family against all odds. The family reaches an uncomfortable impasse. Ernestine graduates from high school. She rejects her father's offer of a job as a cashier at the bakery. She goes to Harlem to follow in Lily's footsteps. She devotes her life to political activism and her family. Lily is found dead in Florida. Ermina gets pregnant while still in high school. Godfrey and Gerte live out the rest of their lives in Brooklyn.

Character Description
Godfrey Crump, 35

Ernestine says, "Death nearly crippled my father . . . taking away his ability to walk at will. Death made him wail like a god-awful banshee." Death clipped his tongue and put his temper to rest. He weeps at night. Death drives him to seek solace in Father Divine, whose teachings Godfrey can repeat by rote.

He wears an impeccably pressed suit every day. His appearance is always neat and well assembled. He brings home sweets for his girls in his pockets. He has a box under his chair, and it holds questions that he intends to ask Father Divine when he finally meets him. He also sends questions to the father in the *New Day Journal* and waits for the answers, which hardly ever come.

Given Circumstances

Who are they? Godfrey is talking to Lily, his sister-in-law and former lover.

Where are they? The living room of Godfrey's Brooklyn apartment.

When does this take place? 1950.

Why are they there? Lily has moved in with the family and just came home drunk.

What is the pre-beat? Lily kisses Godfrey, and he momentarily gives in.

Questions

1. How long had Godfey and Sandra been married?
2. Was it a happy marriage?
3. How did he hear of Father Divine?
4. What is it about Father Divine's preaching that provides Godfrey peace?
5. What are some of the questions he puts in the box for the Father?
6. How is Brooklyn different from Pensacola?
7. What was America like for a black man in 1950 in each of these locations?
8. What does Godfrey like about being a baker?
9. What does Lily look like?

10. What does she remind him of?
11. What does she make him feel?
12. Why does he let her stay?
13. What do his girls look like?
14. Does Godfrey miss drinking?
15. Why does he take so much pride in his appearance?

Late: A Cowboy Song
Sarah Ruhl

CRICK

Because I've always wanted to be a museum guard.

Because I've always loved paintings.

Because I've always thought that paintings should be in a person's house and not in a museum.

Don't get me wrong. I *do* want paintings to be in a museum.

And I swear to protect them. I would never remove one. Or touch one.

I promise to guard them and uphold all the regulations.

I've always wanted to be a museum guard. My whole life long.

Because how could you really look at a painting and love it and understand it if you see it for five minutes—you've got to look at it the whole day long. Maybe for your whole life long.

I'll be the best museum guard you've ever seen. I will.

I'm going to have a baby. I'm going to be the best father and the best museum guard you've ever seen.

A pause while the museum interviewer asks: why's your name Crick?

Oh, yeah, people are always asking me that.

My father named me after the creek I was conceived near.

Sort of a funny name, I know.

I always wished I were named John or Mark or something like that.

My wife and I won't make the same mistake with our baby.

We're naming it Jill, if it's a girl.

My wife—she wanted to name it Blue—but I said no honey—the kids at school will make fun of it. Our child should have a nice old-fashioned name out of the Bible like Jill.

A *pause while the museum interviewer speaks.*

Oh? Really? Maybe it's the translation I read.

A *pause while the museum interviewer speaks.*

Really? I do. Well, that's wonderful. Thank you. I can't wait to start.

Analysis: Late: *A Cowboy Song*

Type: Seriocomic
Synopsis

Crick and Mary live together in Pittsburgh, Pennsylvania. They have been a couple since they were eight years old. They lead a pretty normal life. Mary is the breadwinner. Crick, aside from a love of art, seems to have no real goals.

Things change the day Mary runs into Red, a female acquaintance from high school. The two women have coffee together at Green Shutters, a local Chinese restaurant. Red is a cowboy. The two women become fast friends and meet regularly, against Crick's wishes.

Mary, already struggling with how to be a grown-up, finds herself pregnant. Although Crick's first response is to say they should get married, Mary still has to pry a proposal out of him. Every conversation between Crick and Mary, no matter how unimportant, quickly devolves into a heated negotiation. There is something childlike about Crick. He has demands that need to be immediately met. He also always needs to get the last word in. He needs to win. When this happens, he's placated. With the baby on the way, Crick heads out to find a job. His love of art leads him to the art museum where he lands a job as security guard.

Crick likes things the way they are. He enjoys their life together and is looking forward to the baby coming. Mary is dissatisfied. She gets a fortune cookie that says: your onion is someone else's water lily. She thinks Crick might be her onion, but she doesn't have the strength, or the will, to leave him. She believes she needs to stick it out with him.

Mary finds herself pulling away from him more and more. Finally the baby is born and it has two sets of genitalia. The doctors perform minor surgery to remove the male genitalia. They still can't agree on a name. Mary insists on calling her Blue.

The baby does not help the relationship. Mary continues to see Red. Crick loses his job for touching a painting. Mary finally leaves with Blue, even though her future seems uncertain.

Character Description

Crick Thorndigger, 30s

Crick is charming, fragile, and childlike. He is a great lover of art and especially obsessed with modernism. He and Mary have been a couple since they were eight years old. They both share the same birthday, and he sees their love as fate.

Now they live together. Mary works all day. Crick cooks dinner and leaves a messy kitchen when he's done. When Mary comes home, he wants her all to himself. He wants Mary to tell him all about her day so that he can imagine it, "every moment—like a beautifully detailed painting—the kind a Russian might paint on a hollowed egg."

He believes that in a fair society, people with more money should give to those with less. He convinces Mary to give him $500 from her savings, and then he buys her/them a painting with the money. He thinks that it's an investment and will, one day, appreciate in value.

Crick watches *It's a Wonderful Life* over and over again. He has a dream of perfect family but lacks the skills to realize it. He's intensely jealous of Red, to the point where he reads Mary's journal to learn more about the relationship.

Given Circumstances

Who are they? Crick is interviewing for a position as art museum security guard.

Where are they? An art museum in Pittsburgh.

When does this take place? The present.

Why are they there? Crick and Mary are expecting a child, and he needs to find a job.

What is the pre-beat? Crick and Mary have decided to marry, and if they're going to go ahead and have the baby, Crick needs a job.

Questions

1. How does Crick know so much about art?
2. What does he find so intriguing about paintings?
3. Why doesn't he put his knowledge toward finding a job?
4. Does he really *want* a job?
5. Is money important to Crick, or a necessary evil?
6. What does he do all day?
7. What does Mary look like?
8. What does Crick love about her?
9. Does he want to be a dad? Why?
10. What was his home life like growing up?
11. What museum is he interviewing in?
12. How did he learn about the position?
13. What does the interviewer look like?
14. Why does he watch *It's a Wonderful Life* over and over?
15. What does he find so threatening about Red?

The Lyons
Nicky Silver

CURTIS

I'm trying to figure out why you would lie.

No. No, I don't mean about the leak. I mean about everything.

I don't think there is anyone named Dawn.

I think I know why.

I think you lied, I think you invented her to *avoid* me. I mean, you wanted the sale. You want me to call my agent, to find you an agent. And I think, you thought, if I thought you were gay, you might be expected to do things. With me. So you found a way to make all of that moot. I don't blame you. Not really. Although it was stupid. It was pointless. Because nothing would have happened.

I think your name is Brian Hutchins. And you live at 163 West 83rd Street. You live on the sixth floor, in the front apartment. And you date men. I think you had sex, last night, with a man. Dark hair. Maybe Spanish. He was wearing a red sweatshirt. He was there from eight-thirty, until ten-thirty. You had sex, and then he left. He got in a taxi. And you watched the news. Until you went to bed.

I'm just someone who happens to live at 164 West 83rd Street. On the sixth floor . . . In the front apartment.

Analysis: *The Lyons*

Type: Dramatic
Synopsis

Ben Lyons, family patriarch, lies dying in an NYC hospital. Rita, his wife, sits at his side reading home décor magazines and deciding on how to redecorate the living room once he passes away.

Rita wants a new beginning. Ben is cancer-ridden throughout his body. He is thinking about his life, his past, his family, and his father. He has taken to cursing a lot. He doesn't have much time left. Rita has recently called their children, Lisa and Curtis, to come see him, not divulging the critical nature of the situation.

Lisa, a divorced recovering alcoholic with two children, arrives first with a small plant. She is devastated by the news. She's furious that her mother has known for months and only just told her. She tries to think of good memories of her and her father to share before he dies, but she has none. Rita asks Lisa to bring the children and live with her for a while once Ben dies. Lisa doesn't really respond.

Curtis arrives next with a (much larger) potted plant. He and Ben have never been close, and the meeting is awkward. This is the first time the four of them have been together in quite some time. Curtis makes an excuse as to why his boyfriend, Peter, isn't there. Rita asks him to come live with her once Ben passes, since Lisa didn't answer.

The situation turns even more darkly comic as family secrets spill out: Lisa's ex-husband, whom she may be reconciling with, used to hit her. Curtis made up all his boyfriends to keep his mom off his back. These revelations cause Lisa to drink again and Curtis to storm out.

Curtis arranges a meeting with a realtor who lives across the street from him, and whom he is attracted to, pretending he wants to see an apartment. When he reveals the truth of this meeting, the realtor beats him up badly. Curtis is then admitted into the hospital, his spleen removed. Ben dies. Lisa begins seeing a man who is dying of lymphoma. Rita runs off with a man, with little care or need of her children. Curtis opens up just a little and accepts some comfort from the nurse.

Character Description
Curtis Lyons, 30s

Curtis, originally named Hilly after Ben's father, changed his name. Hilly Lyons allegedly sold Zyklon B to Nazis during World War II. Curtis is gay but has never really been in a relationship. He has made up boyfriends over the course of his life so that his mother doesn't push him into setups with strangers. His current made-up boyfriend is named Peter, and they have been together for three years. He has even had friends pose as Peter on the phone to convince Rita he is real. Curtis is not at all close to Ben, who despises his son's homosexuality. When Curtis was young, Ben, suspecting his homosexuality, threw away all his toys except for his green army soldiers.

Curtis thinks his parents did the right thing in not telling Lisa and him about the cancer until the very end. He is actually surprised by this act, since they are usually "grotesquely narcissistic and infantile." He threatens to kill Ben by smothering him with a pillow.

He is a (unsuccessful) short-story writer.

Given Circumstances

Who are they? Curtis and Brian, a realtor, have just met.

Where are they? An empty apartment that is for sale.

When does this take place? The present.

Why are they there? Curtis has contacted Brian for help finding an apartment.

What is the pre-beat? Rita calls to tell Curtis his father has died.

Questions

1. What does Brian look like?
2. What does Curtis find attractive about him?
3. How long has Curtis been aware of him?
4. Was he turned on watching Brian have sex with another man?
5. Curtis just searched out Brian yesterday by looking at his buzzer and finding him online. Why now?
6. Why does he confess this now?
7. What is Curtis's apartment like?
8. What is this apartment like?
9. What does Curtis write about?
10. Curtis stormed out of his father's hospital room one week ago. What's transpired since then?
11. What is Curtis's romantic history?
12. Curtis lies a lot. Does he think it's okay to do so?

13. Is Curtis accepting of his own homosexuality?
14. Is Curtis sad his father died?
15. What did Ben look like when Curtis last saw him?

Killers and Other Family
Lucy Thurber

JEFF

Shh, shhh, quiet now. Let it get all quiet in there. Quiet and smooth.

It's funny, you used to be so little. I still see you that way really. I should have never brought him here. Look at you, so big now. Now you aren't someone I know. Though, you're still telling stories.

You strip this all away and you're still a dirty little girl making up a world that is better than the one you're in. You're still my sister. You still trying to write our story with a different ending?

Lizzy, can I tell you a secret? Danny thought I was sick when I saw the girl. I wasn't. It was just the first time I felt awake in years. I know what to do now. Just like you always know what to do. I never knew how you did that. Know what to do. But I do now, baby, I know and I'm finally doing it.

Analysis: *Killers and Other Family*

Type: Dramatic
Synopsis

Elizabeth has left her small, rural hometown. She is in the process of finishing her dissertation. She has a girlfriend, Claire, whom she lives with and loves very much. She has escaped her past and created a new life for herself.

Then, one morning, her brother Jeff knocks on the door. His visit is unplanned. Worse, he has Elizabeth's ex-boyfriend, Danny, with him. Elizabeth and Claire's apartment is small and cluttered with pages from Lizzy's (as the men call her) dissertation. This is the first time Jeff has visited her since she left home for college, even though she has invited him numerous times. Lizzy is furious that he brought Danny with him. Danny hurt her, and the implication is the pain was physical as well as emotional. Jeff, seeming distracted, says they need sleep and beer. It's 11:00 a.m.

Jeff leaves the two of them alone to go to sleep. Danny asks Lizzy to read to him. She has nothing around to read, and so she makes up a story. Danny responds in kind, only his story recounts him going to bed with a girl and hurting her. He says he woke up and there was blood everywhere, but he can't see himself doing anything. Jeff came in, saw the scene, and then fled. Now they need money to get out of the country. Lizzy is the only one who can "make it go away." While Jeff sleeps in the next room, Lizzy and Danny have sex.

Claire comes home while Lizzy is out getting the money so the men can leave. Claire is excited to meet Lizzy's brother and a friend from her past. She asks them to stay for dinner. Unfortunately, her excitement turns into a nightmare. She finds herself trapped in the middle of a war as the past comes crashing into the present. The men use her as a pawn to get to Lizzy. Lizzy admits she had sex with Danny that afternoon. Lizzy tells Claire that she needs to trust her. Every move she makes is strategically planned to get the dangerous men out of their apartment and their lives. The physical and psychological torment they inflict upon each other is almost too much for Claire to bear. She had no idea Lizzy came from such a dysfunctional background.

Lizzy finally gains control and convinces the boys to go home and turn Danny in. She and Claire are left alone, unsettled and uncertain of what the future holds.

Character Description
Jeff, 30s
Lizzy's older brother. He's always chosen Danny over Lizzy.

He resents the fact that Lizzy got out of town and left him, alone, to take care of their mother. When they were kids, he would put their mother to bed. He thinks Lizzy blames him for everything that goes wrong, big or small. Lizzy is the only person he knows with money, and that's why he's here. He wants to take Danny to Mexico. He's stressed and exhausted when he arrives at Lizzy's apartment and needs to sleep.

The perception is that Danny always does things, makes the decisions, and Jeff goes along for the ride. He sees it that he's always cleaning up everyone's mess.

Given Circumstances

Who are they? Jeff is Lizzy's older brother.

Where are they? Lizzy's small, messy NYC apartment.

When does this take place? The present.

Why are they there? Jeff needs money from Lizzy so he can take Danny to Mexico.

What is the pre-beat? Lizzy tells him Danny fucked her this morning.

Questions

1. Has Danny ever killed someone before?
2. The woman Danny killed is someone they all knew and went to school with. How well did Jeff know her?
3. Jeff vomited when he saw what Danny did. What did the scene of the crime look like?
4. What was the drive here like?
5. What did they talk about?
6. How long did it take?
7. Who made the plan to go to Mexico?
8. Why has Jeff not visited Lizzy since she left?
9. Has he been to the city before? What's it like?
10. What does Lizzy look like now? Is that different from when she left?
11. Why is it Jeff's responsibility to take care of their mother?
12. How does Jeff make money?
13. Is he scared?
14. How does he feel about Danny and Lizzy having sex?
15. How does he feel about Lizzy being a lesbian?

Where We're Born
Lucy Thurber

VIN

Let me tell you something about people like us. People like you and me, Lilly. We remember where we came from. We remember what's important. It's the state of the world today, man, when a man can't walk down the street without some nigger or Puerto Rican getting in the way, you know what I'm saying, Lilly?

I'm a goddamn American. My dad worked all his life doing shit. You understand? Slaving. Breaking his fucken back, you understand? To just put meat on the table. And my ma fucking around the way she did. That shit's gotta end. Fuck that! This is my country! I work hard hauling the goddamn cordwood day in and day out. I got some pride. I ain't no shiftless motherfucker living off welfare. I work for a living. I pay for my goddamn beer. I ain't like some people around here who only drink other people's shit.

I'm talking about pride! I'm talking about my father and his father all the way down the line. I'm talking about red-blooded Americans. When it stood for something. When it meant something to say the Pledge of Allegiance at school. Now who am I praying to? Goddamn Mexicans and chinks! Pretty soon they'll be coming up here and I got my gun!

Analysis: *Where We're Born*

Type: Dramatic
Synopsis

Lucy Thurber's play takes place in a small, rural hill town in western Massachusetts where the people own guns and are superstitious.

Lilly Marino is a scholarship-winning college student who has come back home for break. This is Lilly's first time home since leaving. She didn't come home for her mother's birthday, or anything else. She stays with her cousin Tony and his girlfriend, Franky. This is a town of dreamers who, mostly, stay put. Lilly is one of the first of this group to actually get out and do something with her life. Of course, as much as they want to do something, they accuse Lilly of having only rich, entitled friends now that she has moved on.

Tony is more than just a cousin to Lilly. He has acted as her father, her brother, her friend, and her mentor. He means the world to her. But Lilly wants more.

Lilly admits to Franky that she's had a crush on her since she was fifteen years old. She takes advantage of the fact that Tony is sleeping around on Franky, along with the courage only marijuana and alcohol can sometimes provide, to make a pass at Franky. Franky tries to deny her attraction to Lilly but gives in. The two women begin an intense physical and emotional affair. Tensions rise over the course of the week. Drew, one of the gang, senses something is wrong, but the others ignore him. Franky and Lilly can't stop, even though they try to. Lilly keeps pushing buttons until she almost reveals the secret relationship in front of everyone. She finally does tell Tony, late one night, and begs his forgiveness by sleeping with him.

The levels of physical and emotional violence the characters inflict upon each other are deep and lasting. Tony threatens to kill both of them, and Franky convinces Lilly she must leave and not come back.

Character Description
Vin Wright, mid- to late 20s
Born and raised in this town, Vin makes his living by picking up work wherever he can at local farms. He sometimes works as a logger. Vin is not much of a dreamer in this group. He's mostly just trying to earn a living so that he can pay rent, drink beer, and smoke pot. He believes "too much reading will ruin your mind." He supports his friend, Drew, by buying the booze and smokes. He rubs it in Drew's face from time to time.

He listens to music like Jimi Hendrix and the Doors.

Vin is content with his small-town life. The friends spend some of their free time playing pool.

Vin recently went on a date with Sally Howards. He doesn't know how serious it is yet. He's not much of a talker and solves most of his (and his friend's) problems with a beer and a smoke. He is offended by the fact that Lilly once slept with a black man.

Given Circumstances
Who are they? A group of friends that have known each other their whole lives.

Where are they? In front of Tony and Franky's apartment.

When does this take place? The present.

Why are they there? They hang out together pretty much every day.

What is the pre-beat? Lilly tells them a friend of hers drives a BMW.

Questions

1. What does this small town look like?
2. How many people live here? Does Vin know all of them by sight?
3. What does he like about living here?
4. What keeps this group of friends (Tony, Franky, Drew) together?
5. What do they each look like?
6. How physically taxing is the work Vin does?
7. How mentally taxing is it?
8. What does he think about while he's working?
9. Does he ever dream of another life?
10. Why does he drink and smoke so much?
11. What was his family life like growing up?
12. Where does he live now?
13. Who is Lilly to him?
14. Why does he get so angry at Lilly for having friends with money?
15. What's so urgent about this monologue?

Women's Monologues

Swimming in the Shallows
Adam Bock

DONNA

I just think it'd be nice if me and Carla Carla were married and you and whoever with a last name were married and we could go camping. All four of us.

And in order for that to happen clearly I have to quit smoking and you have to go out with someone for more than three weeks.

I know what I'm going to do. I'm going to quit smoking. And I'm finding you a boyfriend. Carla Carla will marry me. I'm going to be so irritable.

I asked everyone I know how to quit smoking and here's the list. Hypnosis. Smokenders. The patch the gum. Tried'm tried'm. Willpower ha. Eat carrots because if you don't you'll blow up like a whale. That's from Sandy who's kinda (*"Chubby" gesture*) but at least she doesn't smoke. Read up on lung cancer. Thank you. Pray to Jesus. Exercise. Put Carla Carla's picture on the cigarette pack with a rubber band. Just keep saying I'm going to quit smoking!

So.

Today I'm going to a hypnotherapist.

Here's David's number. He's cute single meeting you tonight seven PM at Twig Beach watch the sunset Ok?

I'm going to quit smoking!

Analysis: *Swimming in the Shallows*

Type: Comic
Synopsis

Adam Bock sets up the question of this funny, intelligent, and absurd play in the very first scene: What do we really need in life in order to survive and be happy?

Barb, a nurse, has just discovered that Buddhist monks own only eight items. She wants to declutter her life, accordingly, in order to focus on what really matters. A woman of extremes, Barb is by no means having her first phase/craze. Her friends and family do not take her seriously.

The play tracks a group of friends as they try to figure out what exactly they can live with and without. Barb sells, donates, and throws away her possessions, risking the future of her marriage with Bob. Donna tries everything she can to quit smoking so that her longtime girlfriend Carla Carla will marry her. Carla Carla keeps finding ways to put off the wedding. Nick is constantly falling in love too quickly with the wrong guy. This time, he falls in love with a shark (literally, a shark in an aquarium). Nick and Donna have an intense relationship in which they simultaneously feed and challenge each other's bad habits and addictions.

Bock is exploring what it means to love someone and the compromises we make when we choose to spend our lives together.

He takes this exploration to absurdly epic proportions in the Nick/ Shark relationship. The Shark is, in many ways, an extreme example of all the unavailable, hurtful men Nick has been involved with over the years. Bock illustrates the patterns these people live with and how once they finally recognize them, they can break them and change.

Donna and Carla Carla finally marry. Barb and Bob reconcile when she realizes that she doesn't need to live at such an extreme. The Shark proves he might not be so hurtful after all by living up to promises Nick's other men never did.

Character Description
Donna, 30s

She wants to marry Carla Carla but thinks it won't happen until she quits smoking. The problem is Donna smokes a lot and likes it. She tries hypnotherapy but continues smoking. She joins a Stop Smoking Breathfree class but smokes with fellow classmates in the bathroom on breaks. She gets irritable when she doesn't smoke. She starts smoking menthol cigarettes. She continues to smoke because she is scared Carla Carla won't actually marry her.

She blames her addiction on abandonment issues. She has a bad relationship with her mother, who wouldn't come to her and Carla Carla's house-blessing ceremony. She is pretty certain her mom won't come to her wedding.

She leads tours of the aquarium. She is best friends with Nick. She, like Nick, had her fair share of relationships here in Twig, Rhode Island, before falling in love and settling down with Carla Carla.

Given Circumstances

Who are they? Donna and Nick are best friends.

Where are they? An aquarium in Twig, Rhode Island.

When does this take place? The present.

Why are they there? Donna is venting, trying to figure out the best way to quit smoking.

What is the pre-beat? Donna has decided that she's going to quit smoking and find Nick a boyfriend so the four of them can go camping.

Questions

1. What pleasure does Donna get out of smoking?
2. Why can't she quit?
3. Does she really want to quit?
4. What does Carla Carla look like?
5. What does Donna love most about Carla Carla?
6. What drives Donna crazy about Carla Carla?
7. How long have they been together?
8. How did they meet?
9. What does marriage mean to Donna?
10. How does Donna's relationship with her mom define/affect her relationship with Carla Carla?
11. How long have Donna and Nick been friends?
12. What does she like about him?
13. What drives her crazy about Nick?
14. What does she tell Nick that she can't tell Carla Carla?
15. What is so urgent about quitting smoking?

The Pride
Alexi Kaye Campbell

SYLVIA

Stay. Please stay.

I should have felt relief when Dr. Marsden said that he couldn't identify a reason we couldn't have children. He seemed to imply that if we just kept trying.

But then I started to question why I wanted it so much. A child. Why it meant everything to me. The desperation. Sometimes, I prayed with my whole body. I would lie next to you in bed and pray with my whole body to feel it . . . the beginnings of it. The stirrings. A new life inside me. I was sure I'd know the very night it happened. And I thought it's natural, it's because I'm a woman. To be a mother. So I prayed and prayed and prayed.

But then I realized that there was something else. I wanted a child because I was frightened of us being alone, Philip. The two of us. Just us. Alone.

Analysis: *The Pride*

Type: Dramatic
Synopsis

"Do you believe in change?" Oliver asks his ex-boyfriend, Philip, toward the end of Alexi Kaye Campbell's time-shifting drama. The year is 2008, and the two men, along with their best friend, Sylvia, are at London's Pride celebration. Alternating between 2008 and 1958, Campbell clearly depicts how much life has changed for gay men in fifty years. No longer condemned to live in the shadows or resort to conversion therapy, they can now live out in the open and with pride.

In 1958 Campbell introduces us to married couple Philip and Sylvia. Once an actress, Sylvia is now a children's-book illustrator. She invites Oliver, the book's author, to join her and Philip for dinner. At the first meeting, Oliver shares a story about an experience he had while traveling in Greece. He went out one morning to visit the famous Oracle at Delphi. While there, he heard a voice whisper that everything would be all right. Oliver interpreted that to mean in fifty or five hundred years there will be a "deeper understanding of certain aspects of our nature." He is, of course, alluding to the fact that homosexuality won't be discriminated against. Oliver and Philip feel an electric charge between them.

That scene ends and we are transported to 2008 and a man named Oliver is having a sexual encounter with a man dressed as a Nazi. It turns out that this Oliver has recently been broken up with by his boyfriend, Philip. Modern Oliver cannot stop himself from having sex with strangers. He picks them up online, in the park, in the bathroom. Philip finds out about it and, after a year and a half, ends their relationship for the third and final time. Philip, thinking Oliver is out of town on business, walks in on Oliver and the faux Nazi.

As the play continues to jump back and forth in time, we see the dissolution of Philip and Sylvia's marriage, sparked by a secret affair between Philip and Oliver. Philip breaks off his relationship with Oliver and then violently rapes him. Philip goes to a doctor to seek conversion therapy. Sylvia leaves Philip.

In present-day London, we see Oliver attempt to figure out why he behaves the way he does as his best friend, Sylvia, tries to forge a life of her own and Philip tries to recover from Oliver's betrayal.

Character Description
Sylvia, mid-30s

Philip's wife. Until recently she was an actress but is now a children's-book illustrator. She has organized an outing in which she introduces Philip to Oliver, her boss, and she's nervous about it. She wants them to get along.

She leaves sketches all around the house — the bathroom, the sofa, the fridge. Then she accuses Philip of snooping. She doesn't want him to see them until they're finished.

Philip says she was a very good actress. She gave acting up because she would "*become*" the people she was portraying, enter their lives completely. She had some sort of breakdown, and they refer to it as her "illness."

She thinks of Philip during the day, alone in a flat he's just shown, and imagines he must be lonely. She suspects he is homosexual or, at least, has homosexual feelings.

Given Circumstances

Who are they? Sylvia and Philip are married.

Where are they? The living room of their London apartment.

When does this take place? 1958.

Why are they there? Philip met Oliver for the first time and they all dined together.

What is the pre-beat? Sylvia brings up a friend of hers, Richard Coveley, who she read killed himself recently. She remembers Philip took exception to him, much like he seems to take exception to Oliver.

Questions

1. How long have Philip and Sylvia been together?
2. How did they meet?
3. What does Sylvia find attractive about Philip?
4. Does she find Philip exciting?
5. Why did she give up acting?
6. Does she miss it?
7. What did Sylvia like best about acting?
8. What does Sylvia like about illustrating?
9. Does she enjoy working with Oliver?
10. Is she attracted to Oliver?
11. If she suspects both Philip and Oliver are homosexual, why does she bring them together?

12. Who was Richard Coveley to her?

13. What did he look like?

14. Is she sad about his death?

15. What does she want her home life to be like? What is it really like?

Jericho
Jack Canfora

JESSICA

There's nothing to do, Josh. It's done. We're getting divorced. I *need* to divorce you—it's clear now—to divorce myself from you.

Oh, aren't you big? What a *mensch* you are. Don't you fucking act like that's not what you want. Like it's not what you've been longing to hear from me for months now so you can go off to the West Bank with a clear conscience.

It's not even enough to divorce you any more, it's too late for that even, somehow. You know what you've done to me? You've done it—the exact opposite of what you'd hoped, by the way, so I guess I should take a little consolation in that. For the first time in my life, you've made me wish I weren't Jewish.

It's true, I wish I were Catholic, Josh, I do, I pray to a great big blonde-haired, small-nosed Goyish God to make me a Catholic just long enough for me to get an *annulment*. What a wonderful thing that must be. To annul—to erase somebody like that.[2]

---

2 You have three options with this monologue. 1. You can perform it in its entirety. 2. You can perform it from the beginning to this footnote mark. 3. You can perform it from the footnote mark to the end.

I'm only telling you the truth. What's in my heart. That's all you've been doing to me, right? You know . . . Josh, I have to tell you . . . and I swore I never would—but in the dark little moments, for months now, I've found myself fantasizing what it would be like if you'd been killed with everyone else that day. At first, it was almost subliminal, you know—too ashamed to stay in my mind for long. But then—at some point—and not when you became distant and not when you stopped sleeping with me—not then—only *after* that, only after it became clear that those things were happening not because of what happened to you, but because of who I was, only when you became visibly *contemptuous* of me, of us, only after *that* settled around our apartment like all that grey dust did those first few weeks, that's when I couldn't help wondering what it would've been like if I could have just . . . been allowed to mourn you publicly, once and for all, when the rest of the civilized world was grieving, too. Instead of what I ended up doing—mourning you privately every day since then. It's the opposite of being haunted. Everyone can see you, but I'm the only one who knows you're not there. That everything I loved, your friends and family knew of you, is gone. What I'm saying is, I guess, is for what you've done to us, how you've treated me, you might as well be dead.

Analysis: *Jericho*

Type: Dramatic
Synopsis

Beth, the main character of this family drama, is dealing with the long-term effects of having lost her husband in the September 11, 2001, attack on the World Trade Center. She has been in therapy for a number of years and has just begun dating someone. Overwhelmed by Alec's death, Beth is on antidepressants, and she literally sees her forty-seven-year-old Korean American female therapist in her husband's form.

Ethan, Beth's new boyfriend, is anxious for her to let Alec go so that they can move forward—they've been dating three months and have still not had sex—with the relationship. He invites Beth to spend Thanksgiving with his family. Beth, who still spends the holiday with her in-laws, agrees. The big question of the play seems to be: how to move on without letting go of the past?

Ethan's family is Jewish, and they celebrate at his mom's house in Jericho, Long Island. Josh, Ethan's brother, was also in the World Trade Center on the day of the attacks. He and his wife, Jessica, are in a very tense period of their marriage. Josh wants them to move to Israel. After the attacks he found religion springing from an extreme case of guilt, because he pushed past people while fleeing the building. Jessica wants none of this. She wants her husband back, not this religious fanatic that has taken his place.

The day gets even more tense as secrets are revealed. Josh discovers Beth is partly Palestinian. Ethan reveals to his brother that he's still sleeping with his office's receptionist. Rachel, Josh and Ethan's mother, reveals she wants to sell the family home to Josh and Jessica and move to Florida. Josh and Jessica end their marriage. Every character's state of mind is eloquently summed up by Beth when she says, "I can't stay connected to anyone. Anyone. Or any place. Least of all myself."

Character Description

Jessica, 30s

Wife of Josh, sister-in-law of Ethan, daughter-in-law of Rachel. She loves her husband deeply and has a very good relationship with his family.

Jessica and Josh are at the point in their relationship when little things become big, such as who has possession of the remote control. Josh would like to watch the news constantly, while Jessica likes to tune out from time to time watching *Access Hollywood*.

Although Jessica and Josh are in couples therapy, they cannot find equal footing. Josh seems to be constantly criticizing her. He corrects her grammar. He makes her feel like she needs to justify herself to him all the time. He makes her feel as if she's not Jewish enough. Josh wants her to move to Israel with him, to "stand up to the Arabs," and spends all of his time lecturing her about things like Jewish history and American foreign politics.

Jessica is drifting and knows that the best option is divorce.

Given Circumstances

Who are they? Josh and Jessica are married.

Where are they? The living room of Josh's childhood home in Jericho, Long Island.

When does this take place? 2005.

Why are they there? It is Thanksgiving Day.

What is the pre-beat? Josh is angry with his brother for not telling him that Beth is Palestinian, and Jessica accuses him of racism.

Questions

1. How long have Josh and Jessica been married?
2. How did they meet?
3. What does Josh look like?
4. What/whom does she see when she looks at Josh now?
5. What does the Jewish faith mean to Jessica?
6. What does marriage mean to her?
7. What were Jessica's expectations of married life?
8. How has her husband changed in the past four years?
9. Do they still have a sex life?
10. How long have they been in therapy?
11. How does she handle his constant criticism?
12. How does she handle his family?
13. Has she talked to friends about how bad things are for her?
14. She describes herself as "drifting." What does that mean?
15. Is she excited about or scared of what life without Josh would be like?

99 Histories
Julia Cho

EUNICE

Listen. You want to hear a story?

I went to the doctor the other day and you know how they make you pee in those little cups? I'm in the bathroom and you know usually you never see any graffiti in those bathrooms, they're always squeaky clean, right? But there I am, on the toilet, staring at the door and there's something written on it. Someone had scratched the words right into the metal, like with a key. And it said:

Hit me

hurt me

call me Eileen

Except there wasn't any punctuation. I couldn't figure out if it was a directive *to* an Eileen: "Hit me, hurt me, call me (*brief pause*) Eileen," or a directive in general: "Hit me, hurt me, call me Eileen." It's been driving me crazy. I can't do anything but meditate on the various states of Eileen.

It reminds me of a joke, you know, one of those name jokes? What do you call a girl with one leg?

Eileen. You call her Eileen. Get it?

Well, hit me, hurt me, call me Eileen, I'm pregnant.

Analysis: *99 Histories*

Type: Seriocomic
Synopsis

Eunice is a self-described "bum." Currently New York City–based but she travels constantly. She drops her mother, Sah-Jin, postcards from time to time but never calls or visits—until she finds herself unexpectedly pregnant.

Eunice stops by her ex-boyfriend Joe's apartment to return her keys, and she tells him that she's four weeks pregnant with his child. He offers to help out in any way she needs, but Eunice has already worked out everything through the adoption agency. Then she tells him she is going to Los Angeles for a bit to be with her mother. Eunice leaves without giving Joe her number out there but promising she'll call.

Once Eunice gets to L.A., she finds herself confronting her own tendency to withdraw, coupled with her mother's tendency to withhold information about her past. As Eunice begins writing long letters to her unborn child (including a list of great books and plays to read), she finds a box of mementos. She believes the woman in a photo to be her mother and a young American officer to be a man Sah-Jin once loved in her village.

Sah-Jin unfolds a story in which the young officer, Daniel, came to the village and asked for music lessons in exchange for English lessons. These stories, along with flashbacks of Eunice as a young child, are told in vivid flashbacks.

Meanwhile, Sah-Jin invites a young doctor from her church, Paul, to dinner in an attempt to set the two young people up. Sah-Jin knows Paul is married, but this doesn't stop her. She has grown close to Paul at church, even bringing him home-cooked meals. Paul reveals that he used to watch Eunice play cello when she was young and was enthralled by her talent. They become friends but not lovers.

Eunice pushes her mother to reveal more and more about the past, including the "illness" that made her stop playing cello once and for all. Eunice wants the secrets of the past unlocked so she can decide what to do with the baby. Ultimately, the two women begin to find common ground, although we are left uncertain about where Eunice will go or what she will do.

Character Description
Eunice, late 20s
Korean American, she grew up in an environment where "what is private, you hide." She hates cleaning and gets nervous when things are too organized. She not sure whether there is always a reason for what she does.

She travels a lot but has recently been working as a temp on Wall Street. She is surprised by the pregnancy (four weeks along at the start of the play) but arranges the future of the baby with an adoption agency before telling Joe about it.

She grew up playing cello and won lots of awards but stopped when she became ill. She also stopped after witnessing her father being gunned down in their liquor store. Eunice never told her mother that she was present for that event.

Given Circumstances
Who are they? Eunice and Joe are ex-lovers.

Where are they? Joe's apartment.

When does this take place? The present.

Why are they there? Eunice has come to give Joe his keys back and reveal her pregnancy.

What is the pre-beat? Joe tells her she has a habit of withdrawing.

Questions
1. How long has Eunice been in NYC?
2. What does she want to do, professionally speaking?
3. How did she meet Joe?
4. How long did they date?
5. What does he look like?
6. What did/does she find attractive about him?
7. Why didn't she move in with him when he asked?
8. What does Joe's apartment look like?
9. Why doesn't she want to be a mother?
10. Why does she go to an adoption agency?
11. Did she consider having an abortion?
12. How does her relationship with her mother affect her decision?
13. When did she decide to go to L.A.?
14. Does she miss playing the cello?
15. What haunts her most about the past?

The Language Archive
Julia Cho

MARY

I am not depressed. First of all. I think you should know that.
Depression, to me, is numbness: the absence of emotion.
My husband sees me bow my head and weep and thinks
that this is depression. Sadness, he calls it. My husband is
very reductive. What he does not know—because he has
not cried probably since he was seven and broke a limb or
something—what he does not know is that there are many
reasons for weeping. There is the: I can't believe how beautiful it is, so I weep. Or the: I can't believe how true it is, so
I weep. Or: I can't believe I'm going to die someday, so I
weep. Or: I can't believe everyone is going to die someday,
so I weep. Or: I am marked for suffering, so I weep. Or: We
are all marked for suffering, so I weep.

Analysis: *The Language Archive*

Type: Dramatic
Synopsis

George and Mary are married. George is worried about Mary. Although she used to be an upbeat person, she has recently become
very sad. She seems to cry all the time, whether she's washing the

dishes or sleeping. Conversely, Mary thinks George is the one who is sad, but when she tries to explain why, he won't let her get a word in edgewise.

George has been finding little notes all over the house. Notes that say things like: "Husband or throw pillow? Wife or hot water bottle? Marriage or an old cardigan?" But Mary denies that she's the one leaving them.

The irony of the situation is that George is a linguist. He studies languages, speaks dozens of languages, collects dead languages, but he cannot find the words to communicate with his wife. And so, Mary leaves him.

The language archive where George works is a collection of some five hundred-plus tapes and recordings and remnants of languages that no longer exist. His assistant, Emma, is deeply in love with him. She is studying Esperanto but can't learn it. Perhaps, her teacher posits, she has some psychological block, since "all second languages are learned out of love."

George has invited an older couple, Alta and Restin, to the archive, as they are among the last speakers of a dying language called Elloway. Unfortunately for George, they are in a huge fight and, when they fight, speak only English to each other. They use terrible, hurtful words when they fight because English is an ugly language and only angry people speak it. Their language is "too sacred" for angry talk. They are fighting because Restin hasn't been eating Alta's food and she is insulted. It turns out that he is sick, and once he is hospitalized and treated, they make up. The couple explain to George that "language dies before words."

Mary makes one last attempt with George. She stops by the archive, but he simply cannot find the words to say "I love you." She leaves for good. At the train platform she meets an old man who gives her a bread starter. This man has been a very unhappy baker for many years and is leaving his business. Mary takes the starter and becomes a successful and happy baker.

George and Emma work together for many years but never become lovers. Alta and Restin remain together to the end of their lives, bickering with love to the very end. George finds Mary and leaves her a tape with a symphony of "I love yous" spoken in different languages, but she doesn't return to him. He, after many years, finds one final note from her, but it is blank.

Character Description

Mary, 30s

George's wife. She has become very sad recently, crying at long-distance phone commercials, at nature specials, or at nothing at all. She does not, however, want to talk about it. She has never seen George cry. She leaves George little notes all over the house, but he doesn't understand them. What Mary wants most of all is for George to say "I love you."

After leaving George, she finds happiness by taking over the Blue Tulip Bakery.

Given Circumstances

Who are they? Mary is speaking directly to the audience.
Where are they? She is in her bedroom, packing.
When does this take place? The present.

Why are they there? Mary has decided to leave her husband.
What is the pre-beat? The last thing George said to her was an uncertain ". . . Don't . . . Go . . . ?"

Questions

1. How long have George and Mary been a couple?
2. How did they meet?
3. When did Mary fall in love with him?
4. What does George look like?
5. What did/does she find most attractive about him?
6. Why did she stay so long if he is uncommunicative?
7. When did she decide things weren't working for her?
8. How long has she been leaving notes?
9. When was the last time she was happy?
10. What would make her stop crying?
11. Why can't she just tell George what she needs him to say?
12. If he said "I love you," would everything be better?
13. Has she considered therapy?
14. What is their home like?
15. Where does she plan on going when she leaves?

The Language Archive
Julia Cho

MARY

That's . . .wonderful. To have nothing. To be tied to noth-ing. To be your own. I think that's both the saddest thing I've ever heard and the most wonderful.

Maybe you could go a little further into your sadness. And see what's there. Can you? It's like this: It's like you're in a room. And you think it's the very last room. But there's another, even further. There's a door. Can you see it? Can you open it?

Do you know, how when you close your eyes tight and can see nothing—it's only then there are sparks of light? Go into the sadness further . . . and then maybe . . . There can be light. A kind of light. All I know is sometimes you can feel so sad, it begins to feel like happiness. And you can be so happy that it starts to feel like grief. You can feel so alive, it starts to feel like death. And you can feel so dead that you start to feel alive. And some people—most people—live their whole lives without touching any of these places at all. But I do. And you might.

Did you see it? The door? The other room?

I'm glad you didn't jump.

Analysis: *The Language Archive*

Type: Dramatic
Synopsis

George and Mary are married. George is worried about Mary. Although she used to be an upbeat person, she has recently become very sad. She seems to cry all the time, whether she's washing the dishes or sleeping. Conversely, Mary thinks George is the one who is sad, but when she tries to explain why, he won't let her get a word in edgewise.

George has been finding little notes all over the house. Notes that say things like: "Husband or throw pillow? Wife or hot water bottle? Marriage or an old cardigan?" But Mary denies that she's the one leaving them.

The irony of the situation is that George is a linguist. He studies languages, speaks dozens of languages, collects dead languages, but he cannot find the words to communicate with his wife. And so, Mary leaves him.

The language archive where George works is a collection of some five hundred-plus tapes and recordings and remnants of languages that no longer exist. His assistant, Emma, is deeply in love with him. She is studying Esperanto but can't learn it. Perhaps, her teacher posits, she has some psychological block, since "all second languages are learned out of love."

George has invited an older couple, Alta and Restin, to the archive, as they are among the last speakers of a dying language called Elloway. Unfortunately for George, they are in a huge fight and, when they fight, speak only English to each other.

They use terrible, hurtful words when they fight because English is an ugly language and only angry people speak it. Their language is "too sacred" for angry talk. They are fighting because Restin hasn't been eating Alta's food and she is insulted. It turns out that he is sick, and once he is hospitalized and treated, they make up. The couple explain to George that "language dies before words."

Mary makes one last attempt with George. She stops by the archive, but he simply cannot find the words to say "I love you." She leaves for good. At the train platform she meets an old man who gives her a bread starter. This man has been a very unhappy baker for many years and is leaving his business. Mary takes the starter and becomes a successful and happy baker.

George and Emma work together for many years but never become lovers. Alta and Restin remain together to the end of their lives, bickering with love to the very end. George finds Mary and leaves her a tape with a symphony of "I love yous" spoken in different languages, but she doesn't return to him. He, after many years, finds one final note from her, but it is blank.

Character Description
Mary, 30s
George's wife. She has become very sad recently, crying at long-distance phone commercials, nature specials, or at nothing at all. She does not, however, want to talk about it. She has never seen George cry. She leaves George little notes all over the house, but he doesn't understand them. What Mary wants most of all is for George to say "I love you."

After leaving George, she finds happiness by taking over the Blue Tulip Baker.

Given Circumstances

Who are they? Mary is talking to an Old Man, a stranger.

Where are they? The platform of a train station.

When does this take place? The present.

Why are they there? Mary is leaving her husband. The Old Man is thinking of killing himself.

What is the pre-beat? The Old Man tells Mary he doesn't know what he was living for anymore, since he had nothing.

Questions

1. Where is Mary going?
2. How much has she packed?
3. What did she decide to take, and what did she leave behind?
4. How long ago did she leave George?
5. Where did she and George meet?
6. How long were they together?
7. What was her last encounter with George like?
8. Would a simple "I love you" from George change everything?
9. When did she decide to leave him?
10. Is there any way George could fix things between them?
11. She considers throwing her wedding ring on the tracks. Why doesn't she?
12. Does she like this Old Man?
13. What does he look like?

14. Is she shocked when he says he plans on throwing himself off the tracks?
15. Why does she continue talking to him?

Detroit
Lisa D'Amour

SHARON

This is awesome. It is so awesome. I mean, who invites their neighbors over for dinner anymore?

Really, though. I mean we've lived in a bunch of neighborhoods now—apartments, houses, condos, even a hotel for a little while. We've lived in a lot of places, and never, never did the neighbors give us the time of day. Neighbors. I mean why is that word still in the dictionary? It's archaic— am I saying the right word? Because you don't need to talk to your neighbor anymore. I mean does anyone borrow a cup of sugar anymore? No. You drive to the twenty-four hour grocery.

Because you don't want to bother your neighbors.

And if you come home from work and you *do* see your neighbor, like, getting out of their car or calling their kid inside—wait, what am I saying? Kids don't play outside anymore, they might get seduced by some homicidal drug addict—ahhhh! Anyway, if you get home and your neighbor is out setting the timer on their watering system, then you look at the ground or maybe give a quick wave and run inside. Because maybe you had a bad day or maybe you have pinkeye or something and you don't want to get too close to them. Always an excuse. And when you get inside, behind your closed door, quiet in your house, you make a pact with yourself to talk to them next time, but then things get . . . fucked up . . . oh sorry. I didn't mean to say that. I apologize. I have a sailor mouth. I do. I'm working on it, but I just think there is no real communication anymore, real communication about real things, about that steak or that sliding glass door, or yes, I would love some more ice, but here we are, having that sort of communication and it's just so . . . it's so beautiful.

Analysis: *Detroit*

Type: Seriocomic
Synopsis

The action of the play takes place in the front and back yards of two homes in a suburb of Detroit. These homes are part of a complex built in the 1950s mainly as starter homes for young couples.

Mary and Ben have lived here for quite some time. Sharon and Kenny have only recently moved in next door. Mary invites them over for a barbeque. Sharon explains that they are renting the house from Kenny's aunt with the intention of eventually buying it. At the moment they have nothing in the house, not even any furniture. Mary lugs out of her own home an old, heavy coffee table and gives it to them. She does not consult Ben in this decision.

Ben was a loan officer and has recently been laid off. He's got a few months of severance pay and is collecting unemployment. In the meantime he's starting a website/financial planning business. He offers to help Kenny for free. Mary thinks he isn't working hard or fast enough in getting his company up and running. While they're talking, the picnic table umbrella closes and whacks Kenny on the head, drawing blood. He's slightly injured but otherwise okay. In the chaos surrounding the accident, Sharon reveals that she and Kenny were in rehab together and that's where they met.

That night Mary drunkenly stumbles over to Sharon's home to confess that she's furious with Ben. Sharon asks her if she's considered getting help for her drinking problem, and Mary snaps at her. She breaks down crying in Sharon's arms and then vomits down her back. Ben comes over and apologetically takes Mary home.

The couples become fast friends. Mary invites them over for dinner again. And, as if to make up for her drunken outburst, she cooks an extravagantly expensive meal that she can't really afford. Sharon then invites them over, even though they have no money and no furniture and she can't cook. At each gathering one of the men gets hurt.

Mary and Sharon plan a camping trip but give up on it when their car gets a flat. They come home and have a wild, drunken dance party with the men. Sharon starts lap dancing with Ben. Then she makes out with Kenny. Finally she kisses Mary on the mouth, long and deep. Sharon starts a cleansing fire and ends up burning down Mary and Ben's home.

As they stand in the wreckage of their home, a man named Frank explains that he is the owner of Sharon and Kenny's house. That Kenny's real name is actually Roger and that he has a history of issues. They were staying in the house illegally. Mary and Ben stand looking at the remains of their home, an uncertain future ahead of them.

Character Description
Sharon, mid- to late 30s.
Raised in Tucson, Arizona, until her mother moved them Indianapolis, where she finished high school. She's fresh out of rehab, where she spent three months for substance abuse (heroin, among other things). She and Kenny checked in the same week and tried to ignore their attraction for a month but then couldn't any longer. Upon release, the first thing she did was go to a T.J.Maxx and buy a floral dress and flats. She can't cook at all. She curses a lot.

She reveals that she actually met Kenny at a club eight years earlier in Atlanta. He had an allergic reaction to seafood and was rushed to the hospital. She spent three days by his side and then disappeared, not seeing him again until rehab. She watches a lot of bad reality TV. She works at a phone bank answering customer service calls.

Given Circumstances
Who are they? Sharon and Kenny are a couple. Mary and Ben are their neighbors.
Where are they? Mary and Ben's back yard.
When does this take place? The present.
Why are they there? Mary has invited them over for a barbeque to welcome them to the neighborhood.
What is the pre-beat? They are just about to sit down and eat.

Questions

1. How long have Sharon and Kenny been out of rehab?
2. Does Sharon miss drugs and alcohol?
3. How did they break into the house?
4. Are they living in fear of getting caught?
5. What was her first conversation with Mary like?
6. What does Mary and Ben's house look like?
7. How does it compare to Sharon and Kenny's?
8. Why is Sharon trying not to curse?
9. How did she find her job?
10. Does she like it?
11. Has she made friends there?
12. How much money does she make?
13. Why hasn't she purchased anything for the house yet?
14. How much money do she and Kenny have?
15. What did they bring with them to Mary and Ben's?

Detroit
Lisa D'Amour

MARY

I thought I could just come to you and talk. Because you cried at my house and—I thought that was awesome. That you felt comfortable enough to do that . . . it made me feel like a good host that you felt okay letting go. In that way

You know what? FUCK YOU. I came over here asking for HELP and what is the FIRST THING YOU FUCKING DO? Accuse me of being a fucking DRUNK? I MEAN IF THAT IS NOT THE BLACK CALLING THE KETTLE POT. God, my husband is offering the two of you his services FOR FREE. He wouldn't even blink to ask for payment. Wouldn't even BLINK. And look at you. This fucking yard.

There's not even a single FERN. You've made no effort.

I was hiding behind our bushes. I snuck out the door to get some air. I JUST NEEDED SOME AIR. I needed to get out of the house. And he wouldn't let me. He kept locking the door on me. And so when the commercial came on, I snuck out the front door and just squatted there behind the bushes. He called and called. My toes were in the mulch, I was breathing, I was not answering. Because he doesn't like me, nobody likes me, and I just want to breathe.

And then I thought, "Sharon likes me. She cried in my yard."

Analysis: *Detroit*

Type: Seriocomic
Synopsis

The action of the play takes place in the front and back yards of two homes in a suburb of Detroit. These homes are part of a complex built in the 1950s mainly as starter homes for young couples.

Mary and Ben have lived here for quite some time. Sharon and Kenny have only recently moved in next door. Mary invites them over for a barbeque. Sharon explains that they are renting the house from Kenny's aunt with the intention of eventually buying it. At the moment they have nothing in the house, not even any furniture. Mary lugs out of her own home an old, heavy coffee table and gives it to them. She does not consult Ben in this decision.

Ben was a loan officer and has recently been laid off. He's got a few months of severance pay and is collecting unemployment. In the meantime he's starting a website/financial planning business. He offers to help Kenny for free. Mary thinks he isn't working hard or fast enough in getting his company up and running. While they're talking, the picnic table umbrella closes and whacks Kenny on the head, drawing blood. He's slightly injured but otherwise okay. In the chaos surrounding the accident, Sharon reveals that she and Kenny were in rehab together and that's where they met.

That night Mary drunkenly stumbles over to Sharon's home to confess that she's furious with Ben. Sharon asks her if she's considered getting help for her drinking problem, and Mary snaps at her. She breaks down crying in Sharon's arms and then vomits down her back. Ben comes over and apologetically takes Mary home.

The couples become fast friends. Mary invites them over for dinner again. And, as if to make up for her drunken outburst, she cooks an extravagantly expensive meal that she can't really afford. Sharon then invites them over, even though they have no money and no furniture and she can't cook. At each gathering one of the men gets hurt.

Mary and Sharon plan a camping trip but give up on it when their car gets a flat. They come home and have a wild, drunken dance party with the men. Sharon starts lap dancing with Ben. Then she makes out with Kenny. Finally she kisses Mary on the mouth, long and deep. Sharon starts a cleansing fire and ends up burning down Mary and Ben's home.

As they stand in the wreckage of their home, a man named Frank explains that he is the owner of Sharon and Kenny's house. That Kenny's real name is actually Roger and that he has a history of issues. They were staying in the house illegally. Mary and Ben stand looking at the remains of their home, an uncertain future ahead of them.

Character Description
Mary, mid- to late 30s
Raised somewhere inland in the United States, maybe Kansas or Denver. She met Ben after college at an after-work happy hour. She currently works as a paralegal for a small to midsize law firm.

She has a plantar wart on her foot. She doesn't like cursing. She has dreams of living in a tent in the woods with nothing but a pot and a pan. She was a Girl Scout. She has a drinking problem. When she finally gets invited to Sharon and Kenny's, she looks in every room and in every closet.

Given Circumstances

Who are they? Mary and Sharon are neighbors and just becoming friendly.

Where are they? Sharon's back yard.

When does this take place? The present.

Why are they there? Mary has sneaked out of her house, late at night.

What is the pre-beat? Sharon gently asks her if she's gotten help for her drinking problem.

Questions

1. How long have Sharon and Mary known each other?
2. How long has Mary lived in this neighborhood?
3. What made Mary decide to invite Kenny and Sharon over?
4. Why don't Mary and Ben have more friends?
5. What does Mary like about Sharon?
6. What does Sharon look like?
7. Why does Mary not like cursing?
8. How much has Mary had to drink tonight?
9. Does she have a drinking problem?
10. When did her drinking in excess start?
11. Is she worried about money since Ben lost his job?

12. How much money does she make?
13. How much money do they need to live on?
14. Does she really want to live in a tent in the wilderness with no possessions?
15. What does she want her life to be like?

Detroit
Lisa D'Amour

SHARON

Kenny you are not going to believe this. I am fucking losing it—do you see me? I am losing it! It was the pink jogging suit lady. At our door! Only she wasn't wearing a pink jogging suit, she was wearing shorts and a blue t-shirt. And she came over to ask us politely—sort of—politely if we could keep our dog from shitting on her lawn.

WE DON'T HAVE A DOG. Exactly. And so I said to her, politely, I said, "We don't have a dog" and she said. "Yes you *do* have a dog and it is quite fond of taking craps on my lawn." "Quite fond." Like slicing a razor blade across my face—"quite fond." And I said, "Lady, do you want to come in my house? We've got NOTHING in our house, especially a DOG. Especially we do not have a DOG." And she says, "Listen, missy." FUCKING MISSY! "Listen, missy. I've lived in this neighborhood for six years, and I jog every morning. This dog appeared out of nowhere and started crapping on my lawn. I'm not asking you to get rid of it, I'm just asking you to clean up his crap." And I practically started crying—look at me I'm crying now—and I said, "Ma'am, people have accused me of many things before, but they have never accused me of having a dog. You need to investigate further, you need to knock on other doors—" And she said—her voice changed and she said, "Look, if it craps on my lawn one more time, I am calling the police" and I said, "Are you kidding? The Police are going to fucking LAUGH IN YOUR FACE if you call them about some dogshit." And she said, "AHA! So you DO have a DOG!" And I said, "No, no, no, no, no fucking NO there is no dog here, lady!" And she just shook her head and kind of kicked our plant and said, "Ha, I thought it was fake." And turned around. I mean FUCK, Kenny, FUCK. This is like FUCKED UP.

Analysis: *Detroit*

Type: Seriocomic
Synopsis

The action of the play takes place in the front and back yards of two homes in a suburb of Detroit. These homes are part of a complex built in the 1950s mainly as starter homes for young couples.

Mary and Ben have lived here for quite some time. Sharon and Kenny have only recently moved in next door. Mary invites them over for a barbeque. Sharon explains that they are renting the house from Kenny's aunt with the intention of eventually buying it. At the moment they have nothing in the house, not even any furniture. Mary lugs out of her own home an old, heavy coffee table and gives it to them. She does not consult Ben in this decision.

Ben was a loan officer and has recently been laid off. He's got a few months of severance pay and is collecting unemployment. In the meantime he's starting a website/financial planning business. He offers to help Kenny for free. Mary thinks he isn't working hard or fast enough in getting his company up and running. While they're talking, the picnic table umbrella closes and whacks Kenny on the head, drawing blood. He's slightly injured but otherwise okay. In the chaos surrounding the accident, Sharon reveals that she and Kenny were in rehab together and that's where they met.

That night Mary drunkenly stumbles over to Sharon's home to confess that she's furious with Ben. Sharon asks her if she's considered getting help for her drinking problem, and Mary snaps at her. She breaks down crying in Sharon's arms and then vomits down her back. Ben comes over and apologetically takes Mary home.

The couples become fast friends. Mary invites them over for dinner again. And, as if to make up for her drunken outburst, she cooks an extravagantly expensive meal that she can't really afford. Sharon then invites them over, even though they have no money and no furniture and she can't cook. At each gathering one of the men gets hurt.

Mary and Sharon plan a camping trip but give up on it when their car gets a flat. They come home and have a wild, drunken dance party with the men. Sharon starts lap dancing with Ben. Then she makes out with Kenny. Finally she kisses Mary on the mouth, long and deep. Sharon starts a cleansing fire and ends up burning down Mary and Ben's home.

As they stand in the wreckage of their home, a man named Frank explains that he is the owner of Sharon and Kenny's house. That Kenny's real name is actually Roger and that he has a history of issues. They were staying in the house illegally. Mary and

Ben stand looking at the remains of their home, an uncertain future ahead of them.

Character Description
Sharon, mid- to late 30s

Raised in Tucson, Arizona, until her mother moved them Indianapolis, where she finished high school. She's fresh out of rehab, where she spent three months for substance abuse (heroin, among other things). She and Kenny checked in the same week and tried to ignore their attraction for a month but then couldn't any longer. Upon release, the first thing she did was go to a T.J.Maxx and buy a floral dress and flats. She can't cook at all. She curses a lot.

She reveals that she actually met Kenny at a club eight years earlier in Atlanta. He had an allergic reaction to seafood and was rushed to the hospital. She spent three days by his side and then disappeared, not seeing him again until rehab. She watches a lot of bad reality TV. She works at a phone bank answering customer service calls.

Given Circumstances

Who are they? Kenny and Sharon are a couple. Ben and Mary are their friends and neighbors.

Where are they? Kenny and Sharon's back yard.

When does this take place? The present.

Why are they there? Sharon has invited them over for dinner even though they have no furniture and Sharon can't cook.

What is the pre-beat? Sharon went to answer the doorbell.

Questions

1. Kenny and Sharon have lived here for five weeks now. How well do they all know each other at this point?
2. What do they like about each other?
3. How often do they hang out?
4. Sharon reveals later in this scene that Kenny just lost his job. How does this affect her?
5. Why do they still have no furniture?
6. If Sharon can't cook and they have no furniture, why does she invite them over for dinner?
7. Is it difficult for Sharon to watch Mary get drunk when she can't have a drink?
8. Why was this experience with the jogger so upsetting?
9. Is it difficult to uphold the lie she and Kenny have started?
10. Does Sharon like this new life?
11. Does Sharon like her job?
12. Has she made friends there?
13. How much money does she make?
14. How much money does she need to make to get by?
15. What is her idea of the perfect life?

Living Room in Africa
Bathsheba Doran

MARIE

There was a party once, in Berlin, that Edward and I went to, and the bar was made of ice. And the barman would pour your drink down an ice funnel, and it would come out cold in your glass. It really was something. It really was.

We used to go out a lot. We'd go to lots of places. We'd go and listen to music, or out to the theatre, or to eat, or parties. There were a lot of parties. And we'd go and we'd watch and laugh. At all the strange people.

I'll miss the idea of Edward. An earlier idea I had of him. Never mind. We can do without Edward.

No, we can stay here for two, maybe three weeks after they leave. After that I thought I could rent somewhere in the city. I have some money. I don't think anything costs very much. We can stay there with the children. And I can try and get a job. We both can.

I'll find work. I think we ought to keep the children somewhere clean if we can. They've been a lot better since they've been here. Remember? You thought they'd be dead by now. Some people are lucky. There are women, prostitutes, who should be dead. But they're not. They don't

even have it. No one knows why. People are experimenting on them.

You will come with me, won't you? I have some money.
Nsugo, I want you to be my friend. Do you think we can
be friends? No but real friends? Do you want to try that?
Nsugo and Marie. They met in the big house in a village
in Africa. Then they moved to town.

What do you think? I'm not going back. Edward flies to
New York tomorrow. I am not flying with him. In America,
when I lived in America, it was very hard not to feel like the
world was coming to an end, and the end would be caused
by human error.

Analysis: *Living Room in Africa*

Type: Dramatic
Synopsis

Edward and his partner, Marie, live in a large, dilapidated house
about an hour's drive from an unnamed African city and a twenty-
minute walk to the nearest village. Natives of England, Edward
and Marie have lived all over the world. Edward has come here
now to open an art gallery in a village where there is no running
water. Marie is a poet. Although they live as a couple, theirs is
not a romantic relationship. There are many veiled references to
Edward's homosexuality. However, Edward and Marie love (or
have loved) one another and depend on each other for support.

At the beginning of the play, the couple have been here a few
months but they are blind to the atrocities that surround them.

AIDS is killing people in the village, but Marie knows only that there is a "disease" present. There is a strange screaming outside the house that no one can define. The water is polluted. There is no educational system. There are no jobs. Edward's one solution is to build a pool for the villagers, since they can't swim in the river because of parasites. When a child cracks his head open in the pool, bleeding profusely, the pool needs to be cleared and drained immediately. No one refills it.

Edward and Marie can't see, or refuse to see, the reality of the world around them.

Anthony, a local who works for Edward, is desperately trying to get Edward to take him away with them when they leave Africa. He is good, honest, and a hardworking professional. It is, through Anthony and Nsugo, the cook, that the realities of life in Africa are most vividly illustrated.

Marie is working on a sprawling poem but won't let anyone read it. She chews a hallucinogenic stick to escape her depression and the reality of her unfulfilled relationship with Edward. She finds solace and hope in her friendship with Nsugo, who has two children living with AIDS and two who have died from the disease.

When Edward's eyes are finally opened to the reality and hopelessness of the situation, he decides to pack up and leave as soon as possible without opening the art gallery. Marie, feeling she has nowhere to go, and no reason to go with him, wants to stay and help. It is Anthony's suicide, on their grounds, that forces Marie to confront the awful reality of the world and to flee with Edward.

Character Description
Marie, late 20s–early 30s
A British-born poet, she has "cut herself off from her homeland." She suffers from a depression that makes her feel "heavy." She and Edward have lived in New York City and Germany. She is writing an epic poem but won't read it to anyone but Nsugo. She chews a hallucinogenic stick and reads a lot to pass the time. She is learning to cook and is supposed to spend her days sourcing rugs for the new house. In her new poem she writes about hurting herself, Edward, and other people.

Given Circumstances
Who are they? Nsugo is a native of Africa, and Marie is her employer.
Where are they? The living room of Marie's house.
When does this take place? The present.
Why are they there? Nsugo has moved into the house with her two children.
What is the pre-beat? Marie has decided to stay when Edward leaves.

Questions
1. Why is Marie in Africa?
2. Is it better here than in NYC or Germany or England? Why?
3. What does she get out of her relationship with Edward?
4. What does he look like?
5. When does she write?
6. What does she write about?

7. What form does her poetry take?
8. How does the hallucinogenic affect her?
9. How often does she chew it?
10. Where does she get it?
11. How much of the village has she seen?
12. What is her attachment to Nsugo? What does she get out of this relationship?
13. What does Nsugo look like?
14. What do the children look like? What are their names?
15. Why does Marie want to stay?

Asuncion
Jesse Eisenberg

ASUNCION

Don't apologize, Edgar, I love America.

I love everything that's American! Why do you think I stayed here for so long?

I think of it like a pop song, you know? In a pop song, it's only the good stuff. In a long boring song, like Beethoven or something, there's only a few good parts, and the songs are like ten minutes long. But in a pop song, it's like they took out the best three minutes of the Beethoven and put it into one song. And that's how I think of America, you know? It's like they took the best things from the rest of the world and made a pop song nation.

Analysis: *Asuncion*

Type: Comic
Synopsis

Vinny and Edgar live in a Binghamton, New York, attic apartment. They are not romantically involved. Vinny is a professor at the university. Edgar was, at one time, Vinny's teaching assistant. He started living in the living room of Vinny's apartment soon after graduation. Vinny is a major stoner.

Edgar is young, naive, and innocent. He calls himself a humanitarian and a journalist, but he has no real goals. His brother, Stuart, shows up on his doorstep unexpectedly one day. Stuart has just married and wants his wife, Asuncion, to stay with Edgar and Vinny while he clears up some business involving Asuncion's family.

Asuncion is a beautiful Filipina woman. Edgar puts up a fight about the situation, saying the apartment is not his. But Vinny has no problem with the arrangement and says Asuncion can stay as long as necessary. Vinny and Stuart used to party together and pick up girls when Stuart would come to visit Edgar in college. Edgar wants to know what the "business" is that Stuart needs to clear up, but Stuart won't say. Edgar is convinced that Stuart acquired Asuncion as a sex slave and that's why he's being so shady about the situation.

Vinny convinces Edgar that he should write a story about Asuncion, detailing her life story and how she got to America. Edgar thinks this is a great idea and says he will do so, but without her knowledge. He begins a very conspicuous crusade to get information from her, but he always ends up talking more about himself than actually getting information from her. Meanwhile, much to Edgar's chagrin, Vinny and Asuncion really hit it off, becoming fast friends and, Edgar suspects, lovers.

One night the three roommates drop acid. Edgar compulsively cleans the bathroom while Asuncion and Vinny trip in the living room. Soon, though, Vinny reveals Edgar's secret plot. The two men get into a fistfight that ends with Asuncion pouring hot water on the two of them.

Stuart returns to get Asuncion. He gives Edgar a check and Asuncion gives him the cash she has left, $250. Stuart reveals that Asuncion's family business involved the selling of cheap antibiotics from the Philippines. He was clearing her from any involvement. Edgar is lost to find his conspiracy theories shattered. Vinny tells Edgar to go somewhere with the money. Edgar researches a trip to Tanzania, but as the lights fade he doesn't move.

Character Description
Asuncion Hirschhorn, late 20s–early 30s
Asuncion is originally from the city of Makati in the Philippines and has been in America for two years. She takes three showers a day. She bites her nails. Mariah Carey is her personal hero. She is beautiful. She eats salads from McDonald's and drinks a hot tea she can find only at a small Filipino shop in NYC. Sunny believes in two things: food and family. She met Stuart online. Her parents sent her to America because she started making bad decisions and hanging out with the wrong crowd. Her dad was convinced a change of environment would help put her on the right track. She has a pretty simple view of the world, seeing people as either good or bad. She likes to try new things, like chopped liver on a chocolate chip bagel, which turns out to be not so good. She and Vinny smoke a lot of pot together and have a very flirtatious relationship, but they are just friends. She truly loves Stuart.

Given Circumstances
Who are they? Sunny is Edgar's new sister-in-law. They've known each other only a few days.

Where are they? The living room of Vinny's apartment, where Edgar lives in Binghamton, New York.

When does this take place? The present.

Why are they there? Asuncion is living with Edgar and Vinny while Stuart takes care of some business.

What is the pre-beat? Edgar thinks Sunny should go back to the Philippines for her own good.

Questions

1. What was life as a wealthy girl in the Philippines like for Asuncion?
2. What kind of trouble did she get into there?
3. What is life like for her in America?
4. Where did she live before meeting and marrying Stuart?
5. Who are her friends in America?
6. Why can't she stay with them?
7. What did her online profile say?
8. What did Stuart's online profile say?
9. What does Stuart look like?
10. What does Sunny find attractive about him?
11. What does she think of this Binghamton apartment?
12. Why does she take three showers a day?
13. What does she think of Edgar?
14. What does Edgar look like?
15. What does she want her life to be like?

Milk Like Sugar
Kirsten Greenidge

MYRNA

Her church sound nice cause you ain't in it. Once you sit in it, it all changes, it all switches around.

A chance. Tuh. What kind of chance the church give me huh? Told my mother I was in trouble on a Tuesday, had the minister over to talk to me and your father by Wednesday, Saturday I'm wearing my Sunday white patent leathers and holding Daddy's hands at the altar with that same minister telling all of everybody what kind of girl he thought I was, but how I was gonna make it all up getting married.

I stood up there watching them all nod they heads like I evil itself tamed in white patent leathers. That minister had all *kinds* of things to say about me but I tell you what: wasn't him around here when you all was underfoot, always asking, needing, pulling. Felt like my skin was barely my own—What kind of chance they give me, those church folks? Tuh.

Analysis: *Milk Like Sugar*

Type: Dramatic
Synopsis

It is Annie Desmond's sixteenth birthday. She is celebrating with her best friends, Margie and Talisha, by going to a tattoo parlor. Annie initially wants a ladybug. Under pressure from Talisha, who says a ladybug is silly and childish, she decides instead on a small red flame on her hip. This pull between childhood and maturity is the main theme of the play. The three girls also form a pact on this day, sparked by Margie's pregnancy, to have babies at the same time.

Milk Like Sugar paints a startlingly candid take on the adolescence of African American inner-city youth in contemporary America. Annie's home life is difficult. Her undereducated mother, Myrna, is a cleaning woman who dreams of being a writer. Her father is mostly absent. Her friends care more about which boy has the best new cell phone and what kind of designer baby gear they'll get than anything else. Talisha is in a relationship with a much older man who abuses her. Margie's man is mostly undefined. For these girls, the joy of having a baby comes from the search for unconditional love. They feel unloved, unwanted, and unseen by most everyone in their lives.

Annie, a sophomore, begins a relationship with Malik, a senior. Her friends encouraged this relationship because of his new red Slidebar phone that is "almost as nice as those Blackberry ones." Their first encounter is awkward. Annie, so intent on sleeping with him to get pregnant, can't see that he is interested in more than sex with her. Malik wants to get to know Annie.

A young girl named Keera, a transfer student, enters the play and brings with her a world of hope for Annie. She has a close, happy home life where they have a weekly game night. Keera has a strong relationship with God. The combination of Keera and Malik's influence guides Annie toward making positive, proactive choices in her life. Annie tries to forge a stronger bond with Myrna but finds it impossible. When Annie discovers Keera's life is a lie, she acts out by sleeping with her tattoo artist and subsequently finds herself pregnant from the encounter. One bad choice derails the rest of her life.

Character Description
Myrna, late 30s
Myrna has three children, two boys and Annie. She works as a cleaning lady in a large office building. Sunday is her only day off. Myrna goes into the offices at night and types stories on the computers she finds left on. She does this even though she can barely read. She is a dreamer and says, "bet I could even make movies out of my stories. I love the movies. Life all big in front of me. Blown up. Lose yourself."

Her husband drives a cab. Myrna makes him do all of the discipline. She believes that sex education should be done by the parents, not the school, but does little to explain it to Annie. She doesn't call Annie on her sixteenth birthday, not even on her smoke break, and makes empty promises to celebrate with her on Sunday.

Given Circumstances

Who are they? Myrna is talking to her sixteen-year-old daughter, Annie.

Where are they? The kitchen of their house.

When does this take place? The present.

Why are they there? Keera and Annie wake Myrna up, laughing and dancing.

What is the pre-beat? Annie tells Myrna that Keera is really into church.

Questions

1. What are Myrna's stories about?
2. How many has she written?
3. Does she share them with anyone?
4. When did she know she wanted to write?
5. Is she worried about getting caught using office computers?
6. How old was she when she had her first child?
7. Does she love her husband and her family?
8. What does their home look like?
9. How much does it cost to keep her family going every week?
10. What does Annie look like?
11. Why does Myrna find it difficult to actively parent her daughter?
12. Why doesn't she call Annie on her sixteenth birthday?
13. Does Myrna have a favorite child?
14. What was Myrna's mother like?
15. What's so urgent about this monologue?

Collected Stories
Donald Margulies

LISA

What if it never comes? What if this is it? No, seriously.
What if I'm a one-book wonder? What if I'm not really a
writer after all?

Everything I've tried to write, all these weeks, waiting
for the book to come out . . . I don't know, I've got to come
up with something *bigger* than myself, you know? Out*side*
of myself. I've got to get out of the suburbs. I need to get
away from people my own age. It's hell being "the voice of
a generation."

I've blown the lid off bulimia in the suburbs. Whoopee.
Big news, right? What do I do for an encore? It all seems so
small now, so puny. My whole world. *You* know: disaffected
youth, disaffected parents. Sex and drugs in the family room.
Uh . . . Mother drinks, father cheats. What else? Oh, yes:
Sorority sister makes a pass at a party—too much to drink
and a kiss in the pool. You name it, I've told it all. Crammed
everything I know into a mere hundred-and-eighty-six pages.
And that's with title pages and like a large-print-edition type-
face that I fine really embarrassing.

It's pathetic. I looted my diaries for tasty morsels. My fren-
zied, angst-ridden, adolescent jottings: I stole whole chunks.

Well, the truth is, I'm not so angry anymore—I mean I'm in "treatment," okay?, and moved to *Chel*sea, so *now* what do I do? I've *done* my parents. I've *done* my family. I'm not *angry* with them anymore. *Fuck* them. I write *all* day, allegedly. I don't *see* anybody, I don't *go* anywhere because I'm allegedly writing all the time. My boyfriend's a *lawyer*; need I say more? My *friends* are all boring because they're all in exactly the same place I am. My life?, I have no life. Every little quasi idea that pops into my brain seems so banal, so *television*.

So, I spend my days writing alleged stories about creatively paralyzed women in their twenties who live in cramped but cozy Chelsea apartments.

Analysis: *Collected Stories*

Type: Seriocomic
Synopsis

Ruth Steiner is a noted author and teacher in an unnamed NYC creative writing program. Lisa Morrison is a talented but green graduate student in that program and a devotee of Ruth's. *Collected Stories* traces their relationship over the course of seven years as Lisa grows in talent and fame on a course very similar to the one Ruth took over twenty years ago.

All of the action takes place in Ruth's Greenwich Village apartment. We first meet Lisa at the age of twenty-six. Ruth has asked her over to provide feedback on Lisa's short story, *Eating Between Meals*—a fictionalized account of Lisa's struggle with an eating disorder as a young girl. Lisa is overwhelmed in the presence of Ruth. She speaks mainly in questions, afraid to commit to a point of view. Ruth finds herself hard-pressed to believe this uncertain young woman in front of her is the same confident voice behind such a finely written piece of fiction. Eventually the two women find common ground. Ruth begins to school Lisa in more than just writing.

Lisa begins working as Ruth's personal assistant. Ruth serves not only as mentor to Lisa, but as friend, confidante, and mother figure. Lisa works very hard to please Ruth, who can be withholding at times. Ruth takes pride in being difficult. For Lisa, who only wants Ruth's approval, it proves to be a very challenging—but rewarding—relationship. Eventually Ruth relaxes her guard and reveals some very personal information about her past.

Lisa takes this information and uses it as the basis of her first full-length novel. Ruth is infuriated. She threatens Lisa with legal action. She attacks Lisa's skill, her voice as a writer. She tries to tear her down. Lisa stands her ground, and the relationship comes to a stormy conclusion.

Margulies finely illustrates the very tenuous relationship between mentor and mentee. Lisa's ascent, although guided and supported by her mentor, is also a reflection of Ruth's descent into insignificance. Once the voice of her own generation, Ruth now feels she has little to offer.

Character Description
Lisa Morrison, 30

Twenty-six years old at the top of the play, Lisa comes to Ruth to get feedback on a short story about her struggle with bulimia. As a young writer, she writes from personal experiences thinly veiled as fiction. She did her undergraduate studies at Princeton and views studying with Ruth as a "religious experience."

Growing up, Lisa was the baby of the family. She had two much older brothers, and when they left for college she felt abandoned. Her parents had an unhappy marriage that ended in divorce. She was pampered and pretty but felt worthless and would do anything she could for attention, including hurting herself.

She wants nothing more than to please Ruth but feels sometimes that everything she does is wrong. However, she slowly begins to make decisions against Ruth's advice, and it's when she does that she finds success.

Given Circumstances

Who are they? Mentor and mentee, a good four years into their relationship.

Where are they? Ruth's cozy Greenwich Village apartment.

When does this take place? 1994.

Why are they there? Ruth is reading the *New York Times* book review of Lisa's first short-story collection.

What is the pre-beat? Lisa has asked what she should do next, and Ruth has said, "You'll figure it out."

Questions

1. Why does Lisa write?
2. How "fictionalized" are her stories?
3. Does Lisa write to antagonize her family, or to find release from them?
4. When she talks about coming up with something "bigger," what does she mean?
5. What would writing a full-length novel entail?
6. What does it mean to be "the voice of a generation"?
7. If Lisa is not exactly writing all day, as she implies, what is she doing?
8. Does Lisa see herself as successful, professionally and personally?
9. What does Ruth look like?
10. What has Ruth's mentorship meant to her over the years?
11. As Lisa has abandonment issues, how has Ruth's steady presence in her life affected her?
12. Why does Lisa still work for Ruth even though she's regularly published?
13. What does it mean to have a *New York Times* review?
14. Ruth has already told Lisa the story that she uses for the novel, but when does the idea to use it come to Lisa?
15. How does Lisa feel being around Ruth, in this apartment?

Next Fall
Geoffrey Nauffts

HOLLY

Remember when you first started working at the shop? We'd hang out all the time. Couldn't get enough of each other. And at the end of the night, you'd walk me home. But only halfway. Maybe a block or two further, if I begged. But as soon as we hit 74th and Columbus, you'd turn around and leave me there.

It used to piss me off. I don't know why. I just . . . I felt like you should've walked me all the way. But you'd only go so far. And that would make me want you to even more.

Well, a few weeks ago, after that weird benefit for Katrina victims or, no, kids with the club feet—cleft palates, right. And you were walking me home, telling me that story about how Luke dropped a fan on your face in the middle of the night, and there we were, suddenly, coming up to that same damn corner. I could just feel the dread rising inside of me. Old, stupid feelings, irrational ones, I know, but there they were again. Well, we hit 74th and you kept walking, past 75th and 76th, and before you know it, you'd walked me all the way to 82nd street, and you hadn't even noticed.

You're going places you've never been before, dummy. Who cares what the rest of us think? Just let yourself go.

Analysis: *Next Fall*

Type: Seriocomic
Synopsis

Luke, an aspiring actor, has been hit by a car and critically injured. His friends and family gather in an NYC waiting room for word on his chances of recovery. The cab driver that hit Luke was uninsured and driving illegally. Luke's divorced (but mostly friendly) parents have flown in from Tallahassee, Florida, to be there. Luke's longtime (and fifteen-years-older) lover Adam was out of town at his high school reunion and came back as quickly as possible.

Luke grew up Christian and remains incredibly religious. This has been a strong point of contention between Adam and him for the duration of their five-year relationship. Adam wants Luke to love him more then he loves God. Adam wants Luke to stop praying after they have sex. Adam's last words to Luke before leaving for his reunion were: "I don't think I can do this any more."

Adam also spent a lot of time asking Luke to come out to his parents. Luke never did. Because of this, Luke's parents don't really know who Adam is, and they certainly don't understand his fevered desire to be near Luke at this point in time. As Luke's health worsens, Adam knows that Luke would not want to be kept alive on life support. His parents do not know this.

Geoffrey Naufft's play, filled with humor and pathos, is told partly in the present and partly in flashback. He slowly fills in the details in the complex portrait of a relationship rooted firmly in love but filled with tension. Adam has spent the past five years wanting to be *the* priority in Luke's life and finds himself in the same position as Luke lies close to death. In the end, Luke's parents take him off life support and his organs are given to those in need.

Character Description
Holly, 35

Holly owns a candle store in Manhattan. Aside from candles, the store carries cards and assorted tchotchkes.

She is a victim of trends: she wore a do-rag during her last two years of high school—even to prom. She also wore a snood. She now does yoga and meditation. She is part of a chanting group. She has been to visit ashrams and taken part in silent meditation retreats.

She was at one time a member of an Overeaters Anonymous group. She was raised a Catholic, and her mom took her to the Vatican for her sixteenth birthday.

She has a "weird competitive streak."

Her business is very successful, and Adam is a former employee and a good friend. Luke took over Adam's position five years ago when Adam quit to pursue loftier career goals.

Given Circumstances

Who are they? Adam is Holly's former employee and good friend.
Where are they? Adam and Luke's new apartment.
When does this take place? One year into Adam and Luke's relationship.

Why are they there? Holly has come with a housewarming present.

What is the pre-beat? Adam wants to know what their friends think about the relationship.

Questions

1. How long have Holly and Adam been friends?
2. How long did Adam work for her?
3. What does Holly like about Adam?
4. What does Adam look like?
5. What does Holly think of Luke?
6. What does Luke look like?
7. What does Holly like about him?
8. Does she think their moving in together is a good idea?
9. What does this apartment look like?
10. What does Holly's store look like?
11. Why did she open a candle store?
12. Does she like running her own business?
13. Why does she partake in so many New Age practices?
14. What is her view of organized religion now?
15. Does she feel competitive with Adam?

Crumbs from the Table of Joy
Lynn Nottage

LILY

Ernie, I came up here just like you, clothing so worn and shiny folks wouldn't even give me the time of day. I came with so much country in my bags folks got teary-eyed and reminiscent as I'd pass.

It was the year white folk had burned out old Johnston, and we'd gathered at Reverend Duckett's church, listening to him preach on the evils of Jim Crow for the umpteenth time, speaking the words as though they alone could purge the demon. He whipped us into a terrible frenzy that wore us out. I'd like to say I caught the spirit, but instead I spoke my mind . . . A few miscalculated words, not knowing I was intended to remain silent.

You know what a miscalculation is? It's saying, "if y'all peasy-head Negroes ain't happy, why don't you go up to city hall and demand some respect. I'm tired of praying, god-damnit!" Mind ya, I always wanted to leave. And mind ya, I might not have said "goddamn." But those words spoken by a poor colored gal in a small cracker town meant you're morally corrupt. A communist, Ernie. Whole town stared me down, nobody would give me a word. It was finally the stares that drove me North. Stares from folks of our very persuasion, not just the crackers.

You want to be part of my revolution? You know what I say to that, get yourself a profession like a nurse or something so no matter where you are or what they say, you can always walk into a room with your head held high, 'cause you'll always be essential. Period. Stop! But you gotta find your own "root" to the truth. That's what I do. Was true, is true, can be true, will be true. You ain't a communist, Ernie! Not yet! You just thinking, chile.

Analysis: *Crumbs from the Table of Joy*

Type: Dramatic
Synopsis

Brooklyn, 1950. After the death of his wife, Godfrey Crump moves from Pensacola, Florida, with his two teenaged girls. Godfrey travels to Brooklyn in search of Father Divine, a mail-order preacher, whom he wrote to upon Sandra's passing. The preacher responded in turn, "curing" Godfrey of his grief. Father Divine's letter was postmarked "Brooklyn, NY," so Godfrey picked up his family and resettled.

Ernestine, seventeen, and Ermina, fifteen, are not accustomed to living in an integrated world. Their upstairs neighbors are a Jewish couple who pay the girls to shut the lights for them on the Sabbath. Ernestine, destined to be the first high school graduate in her family, escapes her pain and fear by going to the movies. Ermina is the more assertive and combative of the two girls. Just as the family is beginning to find their footing, they are knocked off balance by the appearance of Sandra's sister, Lily. Lily shows up unannounced, with all of her bags, and moves in. She has lived in NYC for many years, in Harlem, and is rumored to be a revolutionary.

Lily has promised her mother she would help take care of the girls. And she does bring a much-needed dose of femininity and a modern sensibility to the apartment. However, her appearance seems to be more motivated by the fact that she is homeless and jobless. The fact that she and Godfrey used to be lovers further complicates the situation. Lily represents all the aspects of Godfrey's old life that he is trying to escape: alcohol, womanizing, juke joints, late nights, et cetera.

Cracking under this stress, Godfrey disappears for a few days. When he returns, he enters with a Caucasian, German-speaking woman named Gerte whom he explains he met on the subway and proceeded to marry.

Gerte tries hard to build a family against all odds. The family reaches an uncomfortable impasse. Ernestine graduates from high school. She rejects her father's offer of a job as a cashier at the bakery. She goes to Harlem to follow in Lily's footsteps. She devotes her life to political activism and her family. Lily is found dead in Florida. Ermina gets pregnant while still in high school. Godfrey and Gerte live out the rest of their lives in Brooklyn.

Character Description
Lily Ann Green, 35
Sister-in-law of Godfrey, aunt to Ernestine and Ermina. She promised her mama she'd take care of the girls after Sandra's passing. She wears a smartly tailored suit and white gloves. She bought the suit on Fifth Avenue in Manhattan to spite the white girls. She drinks and smokes. She has a reputation as a nonconformist, a "dangerous" woman. She's been living in Harlem and actively involved with the Communist Party. Lily did not go to Florida for her sister Sandra's funeral but "cried for two weeks" over her death. She shows up in Brooklyn with three big suitcases, saying she's an "etymologist."

Given Circumstances
Who are they? Lily is talking to Ernestine, her seventeen-year-old niece.

Where are they? The living room of their Brooklyn apartment.

When does this take place? 1950.

Why are they there? Lily has moved in to help her brother-in-law raise the girls.

What is the pre-beat? Godfrey and Gerte have had a fight, and Gerte threw his box of questions in the air. Ernestine is picking them up, and Lily pours the two of them a glass of whiskey.

Questions
1. What does NYC, Harlem in particular, mean to Lily?
2. What is the Communist Party, and what does their cause mean to Lily?

3. Why is she teaching her nieces about revolution?

4. What is an etymologist?

5. What happened that she needed to leave Harlem and move in with the family?

6. What kind of jobs has she survived on the past few years?

7. Why does Lily take so much care and pride in her appearance?

8. What was her romantic relationship with Godfrey like?

9. Does she hope they'll get back together?

10. What does Ernestine look like?

11. What/who does Lily see when she looks at Ernestine?

12. Why does Lily drink so much?

13. How does she feel about Godfrey marrying a white German woman?

14. What does Gerte look like?

15. What's so urgent about this monologue?

Intellectuals
Scott C. Sickles

HERA JANE

OK, Margot, look. I used to believe that every woman, no matter who she was, had a lesbian inside waiting to surface. It was the bond of sisterhood and the innate aesthetic beauty of the female body and the sensitive poetic souls of women that led me to believe this. You know when I changed my mind? Thirty seconds ago.

There are plenty of women who have revelations late in life. From there, they make tremendous changes. But these women want to be with other women. And, Margot . . . You're not one of them.

Oh, I'm right. If there are two things in this life about which I am certain it's that *The Velvet Embrace* sucked and you're straight.

This whole "experiment" of yours, Margot . . . It's one thing to experiment with your mind. The mind plays tricks on itself, so it's natural for it to want to play tricks on others. But the heart is sacred. It doesn't know good from bad, right from wrong; it doesn't know anything. It only feels. It only wants, and it wants what it wants because it doesn't know any better. It's not always right, but at least it's honest. But when your experiment involves another person's heart, that's when you have to check and see if it's really worth it. Ask your heart what it wants. You'll find out if it's right.

Analysis: *Intellectuals*

Type: Seriocomic
Synopsis

Intellectuals is a comedic romp through the romantic lives of a group of people, all of whom differ in age, class, sexuality, and experience. Sickles sets up a variety of different stereotypical characters and then places them in situations that explode, or sometimes reinforce, the stereotypes. However, he approaches all of these people with love, affection, and humor.

The main couple in the story—Philip, a philosophy professor, and Margot, a therapist—have been married for twenty years. Margot, seemingly out of nowhere, decides that she needs to "explore untapped potential" within herself. Translation: she wants to try lesbianism. Philip, although shocked, grants her a sabbatical from their relationship.

After an unsuccessful stint of online dating, Margot meets Hera Jane at a women's center. The two hit it off immediately and begin dating. The relationship does not last long, as Hera Jane sees through to the core of Margot, deducing that lesbianism is not in her nature.

Meanwhile, Sickles explores the romantic entanglements of a number of other characters as they learn to love other people by learning to love themselves first. They all make a number of mistakes. They doubt themselves and the people they're dating. They all confront the cynic in them and find their hearts.

In the end, Philip and Margot find each other again, not out of need for each other, but out of desire.

Character Description
Hera Jane Smith, 30s

Hera Jane is an African American, lesbian attorney. She is also a volunteer coordinator at the Women's Center, a place where women can meet and just be women. All of these stereotypes are the author's intention, including the names Hera, from the Greek goddess of marriage, women, and birth, and Jane, a simple female moniker.

She is a fan of classical music and, upon her first meeting with her, invites Margot to an R&B recital. R&B, in this case, stands for Renaissance and Baroque music, not rhythm and blues.

Hera Jane is a real estate lawyer. She is politically aware and an activist. She's a Bloody Mary drinker. Her home décor is heavily influenced by a southwestern motif.

She possesses her own set of prejudices, though. She meets Margot's friend Brighton over drinks. Based on his writing, and no knowledge of the man himself, she brands him a "gay, misogynist theater critic." She defends the merits of the play *The Velvet Embrace*, even though she didn't like it.

Hera Jane has had trouble finding love, and although she is attracted to Margot, she handles the revelation of her recent "sabbatical" with great care and selflessness.

Given Circumstances

Who are they? Hera Jane and Margot are on their second date.

Where are they? Hera Jane's apartment on a Saturday evening.

When does this take place? The present, mid-October.

Why are they there? They have just had a disastrous double date with Margot's friend Brighton.

What is the pre-beat? Hera Jane has just kissed Margot, who responds by pulling away.

Questions

1. What is real estate law?
2. What does Hera Jane like about her job?
3. What kind of political activism does Hera Jane take part in?
4. What does a volunteer coordinator at a women's center do?
5. How long has Hera Jane been out as a lesbian?
6. Is Hera Jane satisfied with her life, professionally and personally?
7. What is she looking for in a partner?
8. What does Margot look like?
9. What does Hera Jane find attractive about her?
10. Margot is almost twenty years older than Hera Jane. How does the age difference affect their relationship?
11. When was Hera Jane's last relationship?
12. How does Hera Jane feel about the fact that Margot has been separated for only a matter of weeks?
13. Why did *The Velvet Embrace* suck?
14. Has Hera Jane been in this situation before?
15. What's the urgency behind this monologue?

Perfect Pie
Judith Thompson

PATSY

Poor Mum. After Dad passed away she was dead within 16 months, eh? Cancer of the kidneys. She used to lie on that divan right there, all day. It was my Grandmother's.

Dark green bile coming out of her mouth and the morphine didn't touch the pain Marie it was like hyena dogs eating her body, eating her alive, day after day, night after night and there is nothing we can do. Well one day the pain seems to have subsided, eh. And we're feelin' kinda hopeful, we are all in her hospital room, 'cept Wayne and Roger of course, eatin' her chocolates, readin' the paper, I'm changin' the water in her vases thinkin' how rancid that smells when she takes, like a convulsion. Her face twists like rubber and her body goes rigid and I start screamin'. Marie, they had to strong-arm me out of the room. This was my mother. I kneeled down in the waiting room and I prayed. I prayed so hard to God I went purple. I was certain that she would pull through because I had always believed in the power of prayer and I felt the presence of God, I felt his breath on my face and I was sure he would breathe her to LIFE and there's people running in and out and then my Aunt Nancy, with a line down her face and her black coat over her arm . . . she is standing there and at first I thought she was gonna say "Mum is fine, she is okay and we're gonna take her home" and I thought thank you God thank you for this and then I saw her face. Her eyes, like her pupils these large black holes; And then I knew; I knew I was stupid, simple to think Mum would make it out of there alive and in that moment, I wondered, Marie, if there is any God at all "See I will not forget you are carved in the palm of my hand." That's what the minister said at her funeral. I liked that, I liked that very much.

Analysis: *Perfect Pie*

Type: Dramatic
Synopsis

Patsy and Marie were childhood friends in the rural town of Marmora, Ontario, in Canada. They met at the age of nine, when Marie's parents moved back to Canada from Detroit. Marie was poor and unpopular at school. The other kids constantly made fun of her and picked on her, and Patsy was the only one to show her friendship, warmth, love, and affection. She took her into her life and her family with an open heart. At the age of fifteen, the two girls were involved in a train accident that left them both hospitalized. When Patsy woke up after being in a coma for eight weeks, she found that Marie has disappeared.

The audience discovers bits and pieces of this past relationship told in flashbacks throughout the course of the story. The play begins with Patsy, married with children, recording a tape for Marie, calling herself Francesca. Marie/Francesca is now a famous actress, and she has seemingly left her past behind her. Patsy, on the tape, invites Marie to come and visit anytime she can. She woos her by including one of her award-winning rhubarb pies along with the tape.

Marie accepts the offer and makes the long drive on the same day that there is a gala in her honor in Montreal. The two women spend the day catching up, reliving their past, exploring their similarities and differences, and eating home-cooked food. Although time has drastically changed them both, for better and for worse, their bond from childhood remains strong and holds them together. The accident in which they were both hurt occurred on the day after Marie was raped by a group of boys on the way home from a school dance. She didn't tell Patsy what happened, just that she needed to leave town. Patsy tried to stop her, but the train hit them both.

Few major events occur over the course of the play. It is, rather, a deep character study of two women and how time doesn't heal scars—it just covers them up.

Character Description
Patsy, late 30s
Patsy is a native of Marmora and has not been much farther than Toronto in years.

Her married name is Patsy McAnn (née Willet). She lives in the farmhouse she grew up in with her husband, Ric, and her two sons. She is a housewife, and she is happy with her life.

While making dough and rolling out her piecrusts, she thinks about the past.

Her father died six years ago and her mother sixteen months after that. Her brothers, Wayne and Roger, were upset that the house was left to her but didn't fight it. Pasty loves the house and the property and turned down a seven-figure offer to sell it to a developer.

Ever since the accident she suffers serious seizures. She calls them "the stalker" because she can see them coming but there's little she can do to stop them.

Pasty was the only person who was nice to Marie when they were children.

Given Circumstances

Who are they? Patsy and Marie are estranged friends who haven't seen each other in twenty years.

Where are they? The kitchen of Patsy's house.

When does this take place? The present.

Why are they there? Pasty has invited Marie to come visit.

What is the pre-beat? Pasty serves up a tray of gumdrop cookies just like her mom used to make.

Questions

1. Why does Patsy suddenly contact Marie?
2. How does she find her address?
3. What does the Marie of Patsy's memory look like?
4. What does Marie look like now?

5. How does Patsy feel about the fact that Marie's name is now Francesca?

6. What does Patsy find comforting about her own life?

7. What does making a pie consist of? How much effort is required?

8. How does it make Patsy feel to take care of people?

9. What does the kitchen look like? Smell like?

10. What's it like to constantly be surrounded by her past?

11. Why doesn't Patsy travel more?

12. Is Patsy happily married?

13. Does she like being a mom?

14. Does she miss her mom?

15. Patsy doesn't believe in God anymore but still goes to church. Why?

Perfect Pie
Judith Thompson

FRANCESCA

Sometimes in a flash I am eleven years old again and they're throwing stones at me. Calling me those names and coughing. Remember? They used to cough when they saw me.

On my bad days I think it was something in me. Something they detected? Something that is . . . still there. You know? There was a reason they picked on me, and not, say, Darlene Rowan, who was also poor.

So I walk out of my beautiful penthouse on the twentieth floor feeling this big kind of Dirty Yellow Stain all over me. The Marie Begg Stain. I go to openings, dinner parties, book launches, and I feel that people are avoiding the Stain, when they do talk to me I can feel them wanting to get away from the Stain, I see their eyes wandering and I feel the others are whispering about me, all over the room, and then I think I hear them coughing, they are coughing about me. And again, I am the girl with the running sores and the scabby legs, the lice and the dark circles under her eyes and the crooked teeth. I am Marie Begg. With the Stain.

You know it's funny, I stand backstage sometimes and conjure . . . their faces and I am filled with a kind of electric

energy, you know? And then I go out, like a lightning bolt;
I guess it's revenge on the stage somehow.

   Where are all those . . . people? Are they still . . . around?

Analysis: *Perfect Pie*

Type: Dramatic
Synopsis

Patsy and Marie were childhood friends in the rural town of Marmora, Ontario, in Canada. They met at the age of nine, when Marie's parents moved back to Canada from Detroit. Marie was poor and unpopular at school. The other kids constantly made fun of her and picked on her, and Patsy was the only one to show her friendship, warmth, love, and affection. She took her into her life and her family with an open heart. At the age of fifteen, the two girls were involved in a train accident that left them both hospitalized. When Patsy woke up after being in a coma for eight weeks, she found that Marie has disappeared.

   The audience discovers bits and pieces of this past relationship told in flashbacks throughout the course of the story. The play begins with Patsy, now married with children, recording a tape for Marie, now calling herself Francesca. Marie/Francesca is now a famous actress, and she has seemingly left her past behind her. Patsy, on the tape, invites Marie to come and visit anytime she can. She woos her by including one of her award-winning rhubarb pies along with the tape.

Marie accepts the offer and makes the long drive on the same day that there is a gala in her honor in Montreal. The two women spend the day catching up, reliving their past, exploring their similarities and differences, and eating home-cooked food. Although time has drastically changed them both, for better and for worse, their bond from childhood remains strong and holds them together. The accident in which they were both hurt occurred on the day after Marie was raped by a group of boys on the way home from a school dance. She didn't tell Patsy what happened, just that she needed to leave town. Patsy tried to stop her, but the train hit them both.

Few major events occur over the course of the play. It is, rather, a deep character study of two women and how time doesn't heal scars — it just covers them up.

Character Description

Francesca (Marie Begg), late 30s

Now a successful actress, Francesca (Marie) has spent a lot of time and energy erasing the memory of Marmora from her mind. However, she always remembered Patsy. She makes the long drive out to see Patsy even though there is a gala in her honor this evening. As a kid, she was always late for everything. She was viciously made fun of by the kids at school and, ultimately, raped by a group of boys when she was fifteen.

She hates this town so much that she wouldn't even come home when her mother was dying. Instead she lay in bed, not answering the phone, until she knew it was over.

She speaks differently now. She is mostly a stage actress but has done three "very, very tiny films."

She's been married three times but is single at the moment. She used to have seizures, but they stopped when she left town. She lives "like a barn cat in heat" and would like to die that way.

Given Circumstances

Who are they? Francesca and Patsy are estranged friends.
Where are they? The kitchen of Patsy's home.
When does this take place? The present.
Why are they there? Patsy has invited Marie to come visit.
What is the pre-beat? Pasty asks if it still bothers Francesca, the way she was treated as a kid.

Questions

1. Why is Marie here?
2. What does she expect to learn or discover here?
3. How did hearing from Patsy make her feel?
4. What does Patsy look like now, as opposed to when Francesca last saw her?
5. When/why did Francesca change her name?
6. How does this kitchen differ from when she was last here?
7. Is Marmora the same as she remembered it?
8. What was the car ride down like?
9. When did she know she wanted to be an actress?
10. What does she enjoy about acting?
11. How has she overcome her past?

12. When conjuring the faces of those kids, what do they look like?
13. What did Darlene Rowan look like?
14. What is the gala tonight?
15. Why did she come on this day?

Perfect Pie
Judith Thompson

PATSY

My mother? Oh no. She was as private as a mole. I couldn't imagine my mother ever taking her clothes off, even for a bath, let alone . . . you know it's funny, when my mother was dying her belly was all swollen, eh, from the fluid? And she's lying there, barely able to speak, eh, and she takes my hand and she says to me: "I'm feeling too sexy." I'm like, "What? Too salty?" And she's like "No" she's gettin' frustrated. It took me about ten minutes to understand what she was saying, eh. And I'm like, "You say you're feeling too sexy, Mum?" At first I thought she was just losin' her mind, but then after about a day I got out of her that her insides were like pressin' down on her vagina somehow, right? And causin' her to feel, like aroused. Alla the time.

I felt so very bad when she told me that. It seemed like a very bad joke or something, right? Her being such a lady.

Analysis: *Perfect Pie*

Type: Dramatic
Synopsis

Patsy and Marie were childhood friends in the rural town of Marmora, Ontario, in Canada. They met at the age of nine, when

Marie's parents moved back to Canada from Detroit. Marie was poor and unpopular at school. The other kids constantly made fun of her and picked on her, and Patsy was the only one to show her friendship, warmth, love, and affection. She took her into her life and her family with an open heart. At the age of fifteen, the two girls were involved in a train accident that left them both hospitalized. When Patsy woke up after being in a coma for eight weeks, she found that Marie has disappeared.

The audience discovers bits and pieces of this past relationship told in flashbacks throughout the course of the story. The play begins with Patsy, now married with children, recording a tape for Marie, now calling herself Francesca. Marie/Francesca is now a famous actress, and she has seemingly left her past behind her. Patsy, on the tape, invites Marie to come and visit anytime she can. She woos her by including one of her award-winning rhubarb pies along with the tape.

Marie accepts the offer and makes the long drive on the same day that there is a gala in her honor in Montreal. The two women spend the day catching up, reliving their past, exploring their similarities and differences, and eating home-cooked food. Although time has drastically changed them both, for better and for worse, their bond from childhood remains strong and holds them together. The accident in which they were both hurt occurred on the day after Marie was raped by a group of boys on the way home from a school dance. She didn't tell Patsy what happened, just that she needed to leave town. Patsy tried to stop her, but the train hit them both.

Few major events occur over the course of the play. It is, rather, a deep character study of two women and how time doesn't heal scars — it just covers them up.

Character Description
Patsy, late 30s
Patsy is a native of Marmora and has not been much farther than Toronto in years.

Her married name is Patsy McAnn (née Willet). She lives in the farmhouse she grew up in with her husband, Ric, and her two sons. She is a housewife, and she is happy with her life. While making dough and rolling out her piecrusts, she thinks about the past.

Her father died six years ago and her mother sixteen months after that. Her brothers, Wayne and Roger, were upset that the house was left to her but didn't fight it. Pasty loves the house and the property and turned down a seven-figure offer to sell it to a developer.

Ever since the accident she suffers serious seizures. She calls them "the stalker" because she can see them coming but there's little she can do to stop them.

Pasty was the only person who was nice to Marie when they were children.

Given Circumstances
Who are they? Patsy and Francesca are estranged friends.
Where are they? The pond behind Patsy's house.
When does this take place? The present.

Why are they there? Patsy has invited Francesca to visit.

What is the pre-beat? They are talking about how they would skinny-dip here; Patsy says she and husband still do. Francesca wonders if Patsy's parents ever did.

Questions

1. How has the day been going so far?
2. Is Francesca like Patsy expected her to be?
3. Does Patsy see the friend she used to know in this grown woman?
4. How difficult has it been getting to know each other again?
5. Is Patsy comfortable talking about sex?
6. How did her mother's death affect Patsy?
7. How difficult was it to watch her mother die?
8. What was Patsy's relationship with her mom like? Does she miss her?
9. What's it like living in the home she grew up in?
10. Does Patsy ever wish she had gotten out, like Francesca did?
11. Is Patsy mad at Francesca for leaving her?
12. Is Patsy jealous of Francesca's new life?
13. Does she miss Francesca?
14. Does she have close friends now?
15. What does looking at the pond make her think of?

Killers and Other Family
Lucy Thurber

CLAIRE

Elizabeth, this is insane. I don't believe in this shit and neither do you. People who kill people go to jail. People build their lives and don't give up moments before they get what they want. Sundays are for family, not for drinking. Elizabeth, listen to me, please, I have to leave. I can't stay and be a part of this. I know you–Listen I know you can't tell anymore. Elizabeth, please stand up. Stand up and walk out the door with me. See how easy it is.

This isn't you. I know you think it is. I know you think they are you. But you have to remember you left and came here. Look around you. You made this place. They didn't make it, you did. I've known you a long time too and you've changed. For Christ's sake, you never beat someone to death in a motel room.

He was drunk, Elizabeth. He was drunk, and he's getting drunk now. And baby don't you see that if you stay you're the next girl dead in a motel room. That's why you left, remember? Because you promised yourself, you promised me, you wouldn't end up like that. Please, please come with me. Don't make me leave you here.

Analysis: *Killers and Other Family*

Type: Dramatic
Synopsis

Elizabeth has left her small, rural hometown. She is in the process of finishing her dissertation. She has a girlfriend, Claire, whom she lives with and loves very much. She has escaped her past and created a new life for herself.

Then, one morning, her brother Jeff knocks on the door. His visit is unplanned. Worse, he has Elizabeth's ex-boyfriend, Danny, with him. Elizabeth and Claire's apartment is small and cluttered with pages from Lizzy's (as the men call her) dissertation. This is the first time Jeff has visited her since she left home for college, even though she has invited him numerous times. Lizzy is furious that he brought Danny with him. Danny hurt her, and the implication is the pain was physical as well as emotional. Jeff, seeming distracted, says they need sleep and beer. It's 11:00 a.m.

Jeff leaves the two of them alone to go to sleep. Danny asks Lizzy to read to him. She has nothing around to read, and so she makes up a story. Danny responds in kind, only his story recounts him going to bed with a girl and hurting her. He says he woke up and there was blood everywhere, but he can't see himself doing anything. Jeff came in, saw the scene, and then fled. Now they need money to get out of the country. Lizzy is the only one who can "make it go away." While Jeff sleeps in the next room, Lizzy and Danny have sex.

Claire comes home while Lizzy is out getting the money so the men can leave. Claire is excited to meet Lizzy's brother and a friend from her past. She asks them to stay for dinner. Unfortunately, her excitement turns into a nightmare. She finds herself trapped in the middle of a war as the past comes crashing into the present. The men use her as a pawn to get to Lizzy. Lizzy admits she had sex with Danny that afternoon. Lizzy tells Claire that she needs to trust her. Every move she makes is strategically planned to get the dangerous men out of their apartment and their lives. The physical and psychological torment they inflict upon each other is almost too much for Claire to bear. She had no idea Lizzy came from such a dysfunctional background.

Lizzy finally gains control and convinces the boys to go home and turn Danny in. She and Claire are left alone, unsettled and uncertain of what the future holds.

Character Description
Claire, 30s
Elizabeth's longtime lover. She brings home groceries to make Elizabeth dinner because she hasn't been eating or sleeping much with her dissertation deadline approaching. Claire plans on taking Elizabeth on a tropical vacation when her work is finished. They have known each other since their freshman year of college.

She's from the suburbs of Delaware and grew up in a house with a small front yard and a big back yard. The oldest child of three, she has a brother and a sister.

She knows very little about Elizabeth's past and tries to get the men to tell her stories.

Given Circumstances

Who are they? Elizabeth and Claire are long-term lovers.

Where are they? Their small, cluttered apartment in NYC.

When does this take place? The present.

Why are they there? Danny and Jeff need money to flee the country.

What is the pre-beat? Danny just revealed they knew the woman he killed.

Questions

1. How did Elizabeth and Claire meet?
2. What does Claire love most about Elizabeth?
3. What does Elizabeth look like?
4. What does their apartment look like?
5. Do they have a good, stable relationship?
6. What does Claire do for a living?
7. Does she enjoy her job?
8. Has she always been curious about Elizabeth's past?
9. What are her initial impressions of Jeff and Danny?
10. What do they look like?
11. What are her impressions now, knowing Danny killed someone?
12. Is Claire scared for her own safety?
13. Has she ever been around this kind of violence before?
14. What was her home life like growing up?
15. Is Claire good in crisis situations?

Killers and Other Family
Lucy Thurber

ELIZABETH

Danny listen, I want you to go home. I want you to go home and turn yourself in, Danny, do you hear me?

There is some shit, you know. At least you know it. You won't be the first guy to go to jail. We know plenty of guys . . . I guess if you swallow enough of the shit, you become the shit. Right? I mean, I guess after a while you can't tell the difference no more. I got no home left anymore. You're lucky. You still get to go back. Woods and fresh air. Real quiet. Sweet soft, kind quiet, late at night. Can't see no lights. Time don't go nowhere. Everything's just the same as it's always been. I love that. Don't you, Danny? Have I ever really told you how beautiful you are? You taste like the country. You taste like everything I ever loved and lost. That's why I could never let you go.

Can you stand? Can you drive? Will you make it? Danny, I don't want you to worry about nothing. You will always see me, won't you? You been seeing me my whole life.

Analysis: *Killers and Other Family*

Type: Dramatic
Synopsis

Elizabeth has left her small, rural hometown. She is in the process of finishing her dissertation. She has a girlfriend, Claire, whom she lives with and loves very much. She has escaped her past and created a new life for herself.

Then, one morning, her brother Jeff knocks on the door. His visit is unplanned. Worse, he has Elizabeth's ex-boyfriend, Danny, with him. Elizabeth and Claire's apartment is small and cluttered with pages from Lizzy's (as the men call her) dissertation. This is the first time Jeff has visited her since she left home for college, even though she has invited him numerous times. Lizzy is furious that he brought Danny with him. Danny hurt her, and the implication is the pain was physical as well as emotional. Jeff, seeming distracted, says they need sleep and beer. It's 11:00 a.m.

Jeff leaves the two of them alone to go to sleep. Danny asks Lizzy to read to him. She has nothing around to read, and so she makes up a story. Danny responds in kind, only his story recounts him going to bed with a girl and hurting her. He says he woke up and there was blood everywhere, but he can't see himself doing anything. Jeff came in, saw the scene, and then fled. Now they need money to get out of the country. Lizzy is the only one who can "make it go away." While Jeff sleeps in the next room, Lizzy and Danny have sex.

Claire comes home while Lizzy is out getting the money so the men can leave. Claire is excited to meet Lizzy's brother and a friend from her past. She asks them to stay for dinner. Unfortunately, her excitement turns into a nightmare. She finds herself trapped in the middle of a war as the past comes crashing into the present. The men use her as a pawn to get to Lizzy. Lizzy admits she had sex with Danny that afternoon. Lizzy tells Claire that she needs to trust her. Every move she makes is strategically planned to get the dangerous men out of their apartment and their lives. The physical and psychological torment they inflict upon each other is almost too much for Claire to bear. She had no idea Lizzy came from such a dysfunctional background.

Lizzy finally gains control and convinces the boys to go home and turn Danny in. She and Claire are left alone, unsettled and uncertain of what the future holds.

Character Description
Elizabeth, 30s
Claire calls her Elizabeth. Jeff and Danny call her Lizzy.

Even though she doesn't live in her childhood home, she pays the rent for Jeff and her mother. She's in the process of getting her PhD. Her dissertation is due in two weeks. Things didn't quiet down in her house when she was a kid until around 3:00 a.m.—that's when she would study. She believes that Jeff, as the older brother, should look after and protect her, but he doesn't. She has $300 left in student loan money and plans on giving it to the men so they leave. She loves Danny but has been hurt by him and is scared of him.

Given Circumstances

Who are they? Elizabeth and Danny are former lovers.

Where are they? The living room of Elizabeth and Claire's NYC apartment.

When does this take place? The present.

Why are they there? Danny has come to her seeking help because he killed someone.

What is the pre-beat? Danny has physically hurt Claire.

Questions

1. What do Danny and Jeff represent to Elizabeth?
2. How does she feel being called "Lizzy"?
3. What does Danny look like?
4. Is she still attracted to him?
5. What was it like to sleep with him again?
6. Did she think about what that would mean to Claire?
7. What does Claire look like?
8. Does Elizabeth like the home they have made?
9. What does their place look like?
10. What is Elizabeth's hometown like?
11. What is Elizabeth studying?
12. What are her plans for the future?
13. Has Danny ever killed anyone before?
14. Is she comfortable accepting Claire's support, financially and emotionally?
15. Is she scared for her safety with Danny?

Beside Myself
Jennifer Wynne Webber

HALLY

Wade? What on earth is your point? Is it that I no longer have to grieve? Is that it? If I'm in the best of all possible worlds, after all. If I'm truly in some happily contented place where I'm better off without my husband, best friend, Scrabble partner, and suddenly—as of late—physics teacher. Because if this is the best of all possible worlds then the others must have been pretty bloody awful. And that's bloody depressing—frightening, actually. That you're telling me I picked this world, this reality, because it's the best. The best thing for me.

Wrong, Wade. I am not choosing this world. I am merely observing it. I'm just sitting here on the merry-go-round of life watching the world go by and it's making me more nauseous too, if you're interested, because at the moment, all I see is that I'm here alone. And seeing is believing, right?

The best of all possible worlds.

I'm sorry if those comforting words of yours aren't having quite the desired effect on me. The expression just smacks too much of cynicism for me. I read Voltaire as an undergrad—I can't help myself.

Analysis: *Beside Myself*

Type: Dramatic
Synopsis

Hally is alone on the deck of her twenty-seven-foot sailboat. She is drinking champagne and jumping up and down, "renouncing all ground."

Hally has recently lost Wade, her husband, in an accident. She has decided to live the dream they had planned to live together. She leaves her job and buys a secondhand boat, originally named *Braveheart*. Hally repaints/renames the boat *Kingfisher*. Wade appears to Hally as a ghost but also in the form of a marina maintenance worker named Wally and a four-year-old girl named Hannah.

Although Jennifer Wynne Webber's play is short on major events, it provides an intimate and intricate look into one woman's grief and her journey to overcome it.

Character Description
Hally (short for Halcyone), mid- to late 30s

Hally is quick, intelligent, and athletic in build, both mercurial and a force to be reckoned with. She is recently widowed. Her profession is physicist.

Wade's death has thrown her into a serious period of reflection. Her friends and family are deeply concerned about her current course of action. In fact, her coworkers have sent her a letter, fearful that she has plans to commit suicide on the boat. They have deduced that Halcyone, in Greek mythology, drowns herself after being visited by the ghost of her husband. Halcyone then comes back to life as a bird, the Kingfisher.

Hally has spent her life living in landlocked Saskatoon in a deadly quiet two-story house.

Never close with her in-laws, Hally recounts the scene for Wade in which she tells them she's leaving. She said to them: "I don't want you to be here for me. You were never that fond of me; I don't expect you to suddenly start feeling differently now. You have your own lives to get on with."

Everyone thinks she's gone crazy, and when she sells the house for a ridiculously low price, gives away all their earthly possessions, and buys they boat, they're convinced of it. She has gotten rid of anything she couldn't fit into the car.

Hally doesn't even know how to sail.

The play is broken up into three parts: Observations, Hypothesis, and Experiments. Webber shows how Hally attempts to break out of her grief and into her life.

"I've learned," Hally says. "I'm focusing on beginnings, not endings."

Given Circumstances

Who are they? Hally is talking to the ghost of Wade, her recently deceased husband.

Where are they? The deck of Hally's boat in a marina in British Columbia.

When does this take place? The present.

Why are they there? Hally is attempting to live the dream she and Wade had.

What is the pre-beat? Wade says he is in the best of all possible worlds, leaving Hally to wonder where that leaves her.

Questions

1. How long were Hally and Wade a couple?
2. How did they meet?
3. What did/does Wade look like?
4. How did Wade die?
5. How long has it been since his death?
6. What did Hally love most about Wade?
7. What was their life together like?
8. Was she ever close with her in-laws?
9. Does Hally have surviving family? What has their response been?
10. Why does it mean to be a physicist?
11. What fascinates Hally most about her profession?
12. What does this boat look like?
13. Why change the name from *Braveheart* to *Kingfisher*?
14. What does it feel like to give away everything?
15. What is Hally's wish for her future?

BFF
Anna Ziegler

MEGAN

Oh! I'm sorry. I'm interrupting—

Are you OK?

If you want, I can leave. There might be another open room. If you want privacy.

I guess you're having a rough day too. I know I shouldn't say it; we've barely just met, but you'd think by my age, I'd have found a way to get over PMS, huh? But no. I'm as pissed off as ever. Now you definitely want me to leave, right? What an introduction. Megan. My name is Megan. And you? Do you have one? I just started yoga. I find it incredibly calming. My therapist says I talk so much that I need to find something I can do in silence. So what do I do? I find you! There were other empty rooms. Don't tell.

It just seemed so much nicer than going to the gym. I hate those machines, the way you strap in and stay there for forty-five minutes. It's like your brain's on hold while your body sweats. It's unnatural. This is the closest I could come. I like to take walks, really. But my doctor doesn't think it's cardiovascular enough. Let me know if you want me to be quiet. I can do that. I am capable.

I mean, it's been such a day already. What a breath of fresh air, huh? Just chatting. I swear, if I have to look another woman in the eye and ask her whether she's menstruating. God help me.

No—I'm a nurse. A nurse. What a world, eh?

Analysis: *BFF*

Type: Comic
Synopsis

Lauren and Eliza are best friends from late adolescence into their early teens. They share their dreams and plans for the future together. Liza is thoughtful, reflective, and surprising—unlike the other girls at school. Lauren is attracted to this and finds that she can be herself around Liza.

However, as the two girls grow older, Lauren begins to mature and grow away from Liza. While Lauren finds herself attracted to boys and yearning to date and explore her blossoming sexuality, Liza does not. The popular girls at school gossip that Liza is either a prude or a lesbian. Lauren begins spending more and more time with them and eventually "breaks up" with Liza. Liza retaliates by throwing herself into running. She loses a ton of weight and is, perhaps, suffering from an eating disorder. She is eventually hospitalized and dies at the age of fourteen.

The scenes of Lauren and Liza's friendship, and its dissolution, are interspersed with scenes of Lauren today. Lauren, now in her early thirties, has never really recovered from Liza's death.

She blames herself. Although professionally successful—she's a marine biologist—she can't find personal fulfillment. When she meets Seth, an attractive, successful man, at the gym, Lauren introduces herself as Liza and carries on this facade with him for weeks.

Megan appears only in this one scene. She is, in Lauren's eyes, a reflection of what Liza would have been had she grown up. It is this interaction that propels Lauren to reveal the truth to Seth. Although it means the end of the relationship, it forces Lauren to wipe the slate clean, take responsibility, and move forward with her life in a way that she hasn't been able to for some fifteen years.

Character Description

Megan, early 30s

She is played by the same actress who plays Liza.

Megan is new to yoga. She talks too much and is looking for silence. At the moment, she has PMS and is pissed off.

She is a nurse. She is in therapy.

Like Liza, she hates water and wouldn't learn to swim as a kid She says, "to this day, I won't put my whole head in. I like being able to breathe. Without breath, how do you feel alive, right?"

In this same encounter, she reveals that she was once in a relationship with a man, Gus, who was really good to her. But she wasn't very romantic, a late bloomer. She got wary of him and stopped sleeping with him, even stopped kissing him, until he just moved away one day. She heard that he married someone else.

Given Circumstances

Who are they? Megan and Lauren are strangers.

Where are they? A large, empty yoga studio.

When does this take place? The present.

Why are they there? Lauren is seeking peace, Megan is seeking silence—and company.

What is the pre-beat? Megan was searching for a studio with someone in it.

Questions

1. Why is Megan afraid of silence?
2. Why does Megan need to talk so much?
3. Is there something about Lauren in particular, or would Megan have walked in on anyone?
4. What does Lauren look like?
5. How long has Megan been practicing yoga?
6. What does it mean to be a nurse?
7. What does Megan like about her job?
8. What is a typical day at work like for Megan?
9. How long has Megan been in therapy?
10. What incident, in particular, provoked her to go to therapy?
11. What does it mean to be a "late bloomer"?
12. Does she miss Gus?
13. Is she lonely?
14. What kind of social life does she have?
15. Does she miss physical intimacy?

ACKNOWLEDGMENTS

To all my teachers and mentors—there are almost too many to name—who had a hand in shaping my view on theatre and how I teach it: Helen White, Jim Carnahan, Nicky Martin, Rob Marshall, Sam Mendes, John Crowley, David Leveaux, Susan Bristow, and Amy Saltz.

To John Cerullo and Marybeth Keating for their support and guidance.

To the people who read and advised initial drafts of the book: Katya Campbell, Dennis Flanagan, David A. Miller, and Saidah Arrika Ekulona.

To all the playwrights and agents represented here, for their permission.

To Mom, Dad, and Joe.

PLAY SOURCES AND ACKNOWLEDGMENTS

Grateful acknowledgment is made for permission to reprint excerpts from the following:

99 Histories by Julia Cho. Copyright © 2005 by Juila Cho. Used by permission of WME Entertainment. All inquires should be addressed to John Buzzetti, WME Entertainment, 1325 Avenue of the Americas, New York, NY 10019.

Asuncion by Jesse Eisenberg. Copyright © 2013 by Jesse Eisenberg. Used by permission of Olivier Sultan. Inquiries should be addressed to Olivier Sultan, Creative Artists Agency, 405 Lexington Avenue, 19th Floor, New York, NY 10174.

Beside Myself by Jennifer Wynne Webber. Copyright © 2001 by Jennifer Wynne Webber. Used by permission of Jennifer Wynne Weber. Inquiries should be addressed to Charles Northcote, Core Literary Inc., 140 Wolfrey Avenue, Toronto, Canada, M4K 1L3.

Bethany by Laura Marks. Copyright © 2013 by Laura Marks. Used by permission of Laura Marks. Inquiries should be addressed to Dramatists Play Services, Inc., 440 Park Avenue South, New York, NY, 10010.

BFF by Anna Ziegler. Copyright © 2008 by Anna Ziegler. Used by permission of Anna Ziegler. Inquiries should be addressed to Seth Glewen, The Gersh Agency, 41 Madison Avenue, 33rd Floor, New York, NY 10010.